George H. _____

NORFOLK HIGHLIGHTS

1584-1881

by

George Holbert Tucker

with a foreword
by
Roy B. Martin, Jr.
Mayor of Norfolk

Commissioned and Published
by
The Norfolk Historical Society
Norfolk, Virginia

FIRST EDITION

1972

Printed by

Printcraft Press, Inc.

Portsmouth, Virginia

In Memory

of

My Parents

Lawrence Holbert Tucker

(1878 - 1945)

Olive Virginia Marshall Tucker

(1875 - 1954)

Acknowledgments

I particularly wish to thank the following for their help in making this book a reality:

The Norfolk Historical Society for commissioning the book, and Mrs. Harvey Lee Lindsay in particular, who conceived of the idea, and who headed the committee that guided its production.

Mrs. William B. Wingo and Miss Janet Fauntleroy Taylor, also members of the book committee, for their help and enthusiastic encouragement.

Carter B. S. Furr, immediate past president of The Norfolk Historical Society, and Edwin R. MacKethan, the current president, for their help and enthusiasm.

Frank Batten, chairman of the board of Landmark Communications, Inc., and publisher of The Virginian-Pilot, who generously permitted me to use material from my twice-weekly column, Tidewater Landfalls, as the basis of several of the chapters of the book.

Roy B. Martin, Jr., Mayor of the City of Norfolk, for writing the appreciative and perceptive introduction.

Lawrence H. (Larry) Hirsch, chief copy editor of The Virginian-Pilot and author of "Per-Verse", for preparing the manuscript of the book for publication.

Robert H. Mason, editor of The Virginian-Pilot, for technical advice on naval history matters included in the book and for his appreciative interest.

William Littleton Tazewell, associate editor of The Virginian-Pilot; and Joseph Willcox Dunn, managing editor; Edwin H. Brandt, metropolitan editor; and James R. Henderson III, a fellow journalist, all of The Virginian-Pilot, for their constant encouragement and support.

Kenneth Harris, Norfolk's unique and nationally-recognized watercolorist and muralist, for designing the colorful dust jacket.

Arthur M. Kirkby, Norfolk City Librarian, and Mrs. Lucile Portlock and Miss Peggy Haile of the Sargeant Memorial Room, the Virginia history collection of Kirn Memorial Library, for their valuable help with research and the loan of pictures to illustrate the book.

Karl C. Edwards and Robert W. Golden of Printcraft Press, Inc., for their unfailing old-fashioned courtesy that reduced technical difficulties to a minimum.

And last, but not least, my dear wife, Elizabeth Braxton Williams Tucker, whose patience and understanding during the actual writing of the book, and invaluable assistance in compiling its index, helped me to complete it in record time.

GEORGE HOLBERT TUCKER

Introduction

The Norfolk Historical Society's choice of "Norfolk Highlights — 1584-1881" by Norfolk's own George Holbert Tucker, with a dust jacket designed by Norfolk's well-known watercolorist and muralist Kenneth Harris, as its contribution to the upcoming celebration of the two hundredth anniversary of our national independence, is, in my opinion, an excellent one, for this delightful book will be a lasting joy for the citizens of Tidewater for many years.

Mr. Tucker's talents as an historian and writer are well known to the citizens of Tidewater through his familiar column, "Tidewater Landfalls" in The Virginian-Pilot, in which he literally brings alive for us the people and events of the past.

In "Norfolk Highlights — 1584-1881" the author takes us on a journey through those years, starting with the Indians who inhabited the land on which our city has been built and ending with Norfolk's participation in the celebration of the hundredth anniversary of the Battle of Yorktown.

From beginning to end this is a fascinating presentation of life as it was from 1584 to 1881 in this area, with particular emphasis on the social history of Norfolk and those who participated in it, including the development of Norfolk's theatrical, church, musical, artistic, and other cultural pursuits in those early days.

As Norfolk had what seems more than a normal share of tragic events for any one city in its early years, these are also covered. But, more importantly, this warm and intimate recording of the personalities of its citizens in those days points out how undaunted by catastrophes were the residents, who always picked themselves up quickly to rebuild and improve their community. What a tremendous heritage they left us with which to face any trials which come our way, to solve them, and to continue to build for the betterment of our city in our times.

Let us hope we will always have a writer and historian with the interest and talent of Mr. Tucker to record the times to come, as well as the times we live in.

I wholeheartedly recommend "Norfolk Highlights — 1584-1881" as enlightening and enjoyable reading.

ROY B. MARTIN, JR., Mayor
City of Norfolk, Virginia

Contents

Chapter One

Before the White Men Came

Indians of various tribes and cultures inhabited the Norfolk area for thousands of years before the arrival of the first white men. Because of a lack of written records, however, little besides archeological evidence of their existence is known today about them.

The earliest definite record of an Indian settlement on land now occupied by Norfolk is found in the writings of Captain Arthur Barlowe, who, with Captain Philip Amadas, headed Sir Walter Raleigh's first exploratory expedition in 1584 to what are now known as the Outer Banks and Eastern North Carolina.

Barlowe recorded in his report to Raleigh, written the same year after his return to England, that the main town of the Chesepian Indians, the tribe that then occupied the area now including Norfolk, Portsmouth, Chesapeake, and Virginia Beach, was Skicoak, "which the people say is very large, though none of the natives have seen it. But they have heard about the great size of the city from their fathers, who reported it takes about an hour to journey around it."

In explorations made in 1585-86 by Ralph Lane, the governor of Raleigh's first Roanoke Island colony, it was also learned that the Chesepians had two towns besides Skicoak. These were Apasus and Chesepioc, both near the Chesapeake Bay in what is now Virginia Beach.

All three of these towns, which were palisaded or fortified with stakes driven closely together into the ground, are shown on the first printed map of the North Carolina and Virginia coastal areas, engraved in 1590 by Theodore De Bry from watercolor maps drawn by John White during Lane's explorations northward from Roanoke Island, that penetrated the Chesepians' hunting grounds.

The Chesepians who inhabited these towns took their name from the great bay, which means Mother of Waters, that washed the northern boundary of their territory. But they were not to occupy it for long after Barlowe's and Lane's reports to Raleigh were written.

According to "The Historie of Travaile into Virginia Britannia," written in 1612 by William Strachey, the Chesepians were wiped out by Powhatan, the head of the powerful Powhatan Confederacy, a few years before the arrival of the English at Jamestown in 1607.

The Chesepians were exterminated because Powhatan's priests had warned him for years that "from the Chesapeack Bay a Nation should arise, which should disolve and give end to his Empier."

It is possible that Skicoak was destroyed at that time. In any event, its name disappeared from the records before the settlement of Jamestown. And by the time Captain John Smith's map of Virginia was issued in London in 1612, the town, or "King's House," of the tribe on what is now the Elizabeth River, was called "Chesapeack."

It is also known that after the massacre of the Chesepians in the 1590s, Powhatan peopled what is now the Norfolk area with warriors of his own whom he could trust, although they continued to be known as Chesepians.

Traditionally, Skicoak, the main town of the Chesepians, was on the north side of the Elizabeth River where its eastern and southern branches converge on the exact site where Norfolk was laid out in 1680-81.

Later historians and archeologists, however, believe that the town was farther down the river toward Hampton Roads, somewhere between the present sites of Fort Norfolk and the Lamberts Point coal piers.

Chapter Two

Exploring With the Smith Party

As far as can be ascertained, Captain John Smith and the twelve Jamestown colonists who accompanied him on his second exploration of the Chesapeake Bay were the first known white men to enter what is now the Elizabeth River to visit the area now incorporated within the present limits of Norfolk.

Smith had previously explored the Chesapeake Bay region during the early summer months of 1608, at which time he almost lost his life when he was stung by a stingray off what is still known as Stingray Point in Middlesex County.

According to the account of the second exploratory trip written by Anthony Bagnall, the surgeon of the expedition, Nathaniel Powell, a gentleman, and Anas Todkill, a soldier, the cocky, red-haired, red-bearded Captain Smith and his party left Jamestown on July 24, 1608, in an open boat equipped with a sail and oars for the trip into country "till then to any Christian unknowne."

Besides the three men already mentioned, Smith's party consisted of Thomas Momford, Richard Featherstone, Michael Sickelmore, and James Bourne, gentlemen; and Jonas Profit, Edward Pising, Richard Keale, James Watkins, and William Ward, soldiers.

Heading down the James River, Smith and his party spent a few days at Kecoughtan (Hampton), where "the King feasted us with mirth."

The English were not above a little skulduggery to encourage cooperation on the part of the natives, as the account shows: "In the evening we fired a few rackets (rockets), which flying into the ayre so terrified the poor Salvages, they supposed nothing impossible we attempted, and desired to assist us."

Throughout the trip most of Smith's men "were sicke almost to death, until they were seasoned to the Country," but that didn't interrupt the dynamic captain's plans. And before the expedition returned to Jamestown on September 7, 1608, he and his men had chalked up all kinds of experiences, ranging from almost continuous Indian attacks to the death of Richard Featherstone, whom they buried "with a volley of shot."

The visit to the Elizabeth River area took place on their way back to Jamestown. This is how the narrative describes it:

"In a fayre calme, rowing towards poynt Comfort, we anchored in Gosnolls Bay, but such a suddaine gust surprised us in the night with thunder and rayne, that we never thought more to have seene James Towne. Yet running before the wind, we sometimes saw the Land by the flashes of fire from heaven by which light onely we kept from the splitting shore, until it pleased God in that blacke darknesse to preserve us by that light to finde poynt Comfort: there refreshing our selves, because we had onely but heard of the Chisapeacks & Nandsamunds, we thought it as fit to know all our neighbours neare home, as so many Nations abroad.

"So setting sayle for the Southerne shore, we sayled up a narrow river up the country of Chisapeack; it hath a good channell, but many shoules about the entrance. By that we had sayled six or seaven myles, we saw two or three little garden plots with their houses, the shore overgrowne with the greatest Pyne and Firre trees we ever saw in the Country. But nott seeing nor hearing any people, and the river very narrow, we returned to the great river, to see if we could finde any of them."

Chapter Three

Whence Elizabeth River, Willoughby, and Two Points

The river that connects Norfolk with Hampton Roads, and three of the city's best-known geographical areas, have names that date from the first years of the Seventeenth Century.

These are the Elizabeth River, Willoughby, Sewells Point, and Lamberts Point, the last three having derived their names from prominent early Norfolk area settlers.

The Elizabeth River was named for the Princess Elizabeth Stuart (1596-1660), the daughter of King James I of England and a sister of Prince Henry Stuart and Prince Charles Stuart, later King Charles I, for whom the first Jamestown colonists named the two capes that guard the entrance to the Chesapeake Bay.

Elizabeth City County, originally known by "the savage name of Kiccowtan," from which Lower Norfolk County was carved in 1637, was also named for her.

Willoughby takes its name from Captain Thomas Willoughby, who arrived in Virginia in 1610 at the age of nine as a passenger on the ship Prosperous.

Once he got a foothold in the New World, Willoughby's rise was rapid. And he was, successively, a justice of the peace, a member of the Assembly at Jamestown, and a member of the Governor's Council. He died in 1658 during a visit to England.

It is a matter of record that he owned a large tract of land embracing the present Willoughby area before 1626, and by 1635 he had built his family "manor house" there. This stood somewhere to the north of the present Ocean View Elementary School near the spot then known as "Willoughby's Point." What is now known as Willoughby Spit, however, dates from the middle years of the Eighteenth Century.

Even during the lifetime of Captain Thomas Willoughby, a series of underwater shoals formed over the years by the action of the waters of Hampton Roads and Chesapeake Bay existed west of the Willoughby manor plantation.

Then, quite suddenly, in October of 1749, the Norfolk area

was visited by a terrific tropical hurricane that did considerable crop and property damage and destroyed Fort George, which stood on the present site of Fort Monroe.

The accumulated sand churned up by this storm caused the shoals adjacent to the Willoughby plantation to surface. And from then on the long curved finger of sand continued to build up until it became known by its present name, Willoughby Spit.

Sewells Point, a corruption of "Mr. Seawell's Pointe," takes its name from Henry Seawell, who had settled by 1629 in Elizabeth City County, from which Lower Norfolk County was carved in 1637.

According to the record, Henry Seawell the elder did "cleare, seate, build, and plant" on one hundred and fifty acres of the tract later known by his name shortly after December of 1633.

With his neighbor, Captain Thomas Willoughby, Seawell was among the Virginia executors of Captain Adam Thorowgood, the leading Norfolk area citizen of his day, when the latter died in 1640.

Between 1638 and 1640, the first parish church of Lower Norfolk County, the mother church of the Episcopal Church in the Norfolk area, was built on Sewells Point somewhere on the site of the present Norfolk Naval Station. And when Seawell and his wife died in the early 1640s, they were buried in its chancel.

Lamberts Point, now the site of one of the busiest coal export facilities in the world, was named for Thomas Lambert, who patented one hundred acres there on the east side of the "Bay" of Elizabeth River on June 1, 1635, when the territory was still a part of Elizabeth City County.

Lambert was an ensign in the Lower Norfolk County Militia by 1640 and was later a major in the same outfit. He was later a member of the Assembly at Jamestown for Lower Norfolk County in 1652, and by the time of his death in 1671 he was the proud bearer of the title Lieutenant Colonel Thomas Lambert.

Chapter Four

The Origin of Norfolk's Name

The name Norfolk as a corporate appellation was derived from the "Towne of Lower Norfolk County" ordered to be established by the Lower Norfolk County Court on August 18, 1680, in compliance with "An Act for Co-habitation and the Encouragement of Trade and Manufacture" passed in June of the same year by the General Assembly of Virginia at Jamestown.

The town's name was derived from Lower Norfolk County in which it was located and which then included the area now occupied by the cities of Norfolk, Portsmouth, Chesapeake, and Virginia Beach.

Lower Norfolk County was originally a part of Elizabeth City County, earlier known by "the savage name of Kiccowtan."

The first court for Lower Norfolk County, then designated as "the Lower County of New Norfolk," was held on May 15, 1637. And it is significant that Captain Adam Thorowgood (1604-1640), the man who according to long-standing tradition was responsible for naming the new country for his native shire of Norfolk in England, was the presiding justice.

Thorowgood, who was Lower Norfolk's County's leading citizen in his day, also traditionally changed the name of the Chesopean River, on which he received a princely grant of 5,350 acres of land in 1635, to the Lynnhaven River in memory of the King's Lynn in his native Norfolk. It is said that Thorowgood changed the name because of the then striking resemblance between the Virginia river and the River Ouse that flows through the Norfolk fenland to the Wash and the North Sea.

Be that as it may, there is another theory as to how the name of Norfolk became a Virginia appellation. Briefly, the facts are these:

On July 5, 1636, King Charles I wrote to Governor John Harvey of Virginia on behalf of Henry, Lord Maltravers, ordering him to grant the latter a tract of land in the southern part of Virginia "as may beare the name of a county and be called the county of Norfolk."

Since Lord Maltravers belonged to the family that formerly bore the title of Duke of Norfolk, it is obvious where the proposed name for the new county came from.

As the king's letter miscarried, however, another letter was dispatched on April 11, 1637, repeating the request for the grant that was finally made by Harvey on January 22, 1637/38.

Even the most casual examination of the date of the first sitting of the Lower Norfolk County Court (May 15, 1637), however, will show that the county had been established and named nine months before Harvey made the grant to Maltravers on January 22, 1637/38.

This more or less leads one to believe that the Thorowgood tradition is correct.

Another argument in its favor is the fact that Thorowgood was a member of the Governor's Council at the time of the establishment of Lower Norfolk County. And this, together with the fact that he was the leading citizen of the new territory, makes it highly probable that he was permitted to name the new county, from which the Norfolk of today takes its name, for his native shire in England.

That the transplanted captain from Norfolk, England, took his position seriously and was not lightly trifled with is evident from a record of the court for the new county that he traditionally named dated May 15, 1637.

This tells us that a certain woman with an overfree tongue who had been impertinent to Thorowgood was sentenced to receive twenty lashes on her bare back for her sauciness.

Chapter Five

The History of Norfolk's Site

The narrow strip of land fronting the Elizabeth River on which Norfolk was originally established was owned by six early Virginia settlers and one mercantile group before it was laid out as a townsite in 1680-81 by John Ferebee, the surveyor for Lower Norfolk County.

For many years it was believed that the Indian town of Skicoak, one of the three settlements of the Chesepian Indian tribe, supposedly occupied the site of Norfolk. But later historians, after a careful sifting of the evidence, have come to the conclusion that Skicoak was on the Elizabeth River closer to Hampton Roads, while the site that eventually became the nucleus of the present Norfolk was either Indian corn land or primeval forest until the English took over.

In any event, the first white man to own the site on which Norfolk was established was Captain Thomas Willoughby, who patented two hundred acres "upon the first eastern branch of the Elizabeth River" on February 13, 1636/37.

Born in England around 1601, Willoughby came to Virginia as a boy on the ship Prosperous in 1610. He became one of the most important merchants in Seventeenth Century Virginia, and his "manor plantation" was on the present site of Ocean View. Willoughby was successively a justice of the peace, a member of the Virginia Assembly at Jamestown, and a member of the Governor's Council. He was also a dangerous man to trifle with.

For instance, in 1646, a little over a decade before his death in England in 1658, an indiscreet Lower Norfolk County citizen who slandered him was sentenced by the court to receive fifteen lashes on his bare back, after which he had to appear in all public places for a time wearing a piece of paper bound to his forehead on which a brief account of his peccadillo was inscribed.

Willoughby owned the original site of Norfolk for only seven years, however, for he sold it on April 1, 1644 to John Watkins, another prominent Lower Norfolk County citizen, who again sold it on April 30, 1644, to a man named John Norwood. He continued to hold the property until March 4, 1649/50, at which time he sold the site to Peter Michaelson "and others, owners of the Ship Huis van Nassau (House of Nassau)." This group, headed by Michaelson, is presumed by historians to have been a Dutch trading company.

A few years later, on February 18, 1653/54, the site was bought by Francis Emperor, another merchant, who renewed the patent for the land on March 3, 1656/57, after which it changed hands again, this time to Lewis Vandermuller, presumably another Hollander. On October 19, 1662, the site was bought by Nicholas Wise Sr., who had the deed confirmed on March 18, 1662/63.

It was Wise's son who owned the property in June 1680 when the Virginia Assembly at Jamestown passed an "Act for Co-habitation and the Encouragement of Trade and Manufacture" that provided for the establishment of a town in each of the twenty then-existing Virginia counties.

Once the land was surveyed it was deeded to the trustees of Lower Norfolk County on August 16, 1682, by Nicholas Wise Jr., a shipwright and a son of Nicholas Wise Sr. The fifty-acre tract, purchased from Wise for ten thousand pounds of tobacco in cask, was bounded on the south and west by the Elizabeth River and on the north and east by Back Creek and Dun-in-the-Mire Creek.

As Norfolk was destined to become an important seaport, it was fitting that a seafaring man was the first property owner in the newly established town.

On October 17, 1683, Peter Smith, a mariner, purchased three half-acre lots from the county authorities. These were in the immediate vicinity of what was to become Market Square, later known as Commercial Place. The site is now part of the property owned by the soaring Virginia National Bank.

Chapter Six

The "Half Moone" Fort

There was a fort on the site of downtown Norfolk seven years before the establishment of the town in 1680. The fort was an outgrowth of the war between England and the Netherlands, during which the latter lost its colonial possessions on the North American continent.

Three years after the British took possession of New Amsterdam in 1664 and renamed it New York, a retaliating Dutch fleet swooped down on a fully loaded tobacco fleet of twenty vessels anchored at the mouth of the James River. After disabling the Eilzabeth, a leaky old forty-six gun frigate detailed to defend the convoy, the Dutch captured all of the defenseless merchantmen, burned five or six of them, and made off with the others.

Six years later a similar Dutch fleet wreaked havoc on another tobacco fleet anchored in Lynnhaven Bay. Alarmed by such daring actions on its doorstep, the Virginia Assembly bestirred itself to pass laws to provide for the protection of its people and commerce.

An act of 1667 had already authorized the construction of five forts on the James, Nansemond, York, Rappahannock and Potomac rivers. And after the 1673 attack another act was passed to build two additional forts, one in Isle of Wight County, the other in Lower Norfolk County.

The act provided that the forts be erected at the expense of the county to be defended. And after the freemen of Lower

Norfolk County, which then included the area now occupied by Norfolk, Chesapeake, Portsmouth, and Virginia Beach, had agreed to foot the bill, the justices of the county went ahead with the building plans.

The old court record reads: "It is therefore by them Ordered that it be built upon foure farthing point, being a point of land belonging to the orphants of Nicholas Wise, decd., and that the modell be in the form of a half moone."

In order to cut down on expenses, the justices ordered that every tithable in the county give two days of free labor on the project or "hier others in their Roome."

A Lower Norfolk County citizen named Paul Trige was also appointed "overseer of the work" on which every worker furnished his own tools and food. To put a bite into the law, the justices also decreed that anyone who refused to bear his share of the work was to be fined twenty-five pounds of tobacco for each day he failed to show up on the job.

Four Farthing Point, on which the fort was built, was at the extreme western end of Main Street directly opposite the present Portsmouth Naval Hospital. It was also the same site that was later known as Town Point. The ordnance of the fort consisted of demi-cannon and whole culverns "because our rivers are so wide."

Apparently the fort, which cost the citizens of Lower Norfolk County thirty-five thousand pounds of tobacco to erect, had been completed by October 7, 1680, when John Ferebee, the Lower Norfolk County surveyor, began laying out the nucleus of the present Norfolk.

All traces of the early fort, which antedated the port of Norfolk by seven years, have disappeared. But as late as 1781, when the British occupied the Norfolk and Portsmouth area during the Revolutionary War, professional soldiers of Great Britain erected another temporary fort on the same site to protect the inner Norfolk harbor.

Chapter Seven

The Birth of "Norfolk Towne"

The date 1682 on the Norfolk City Seal, purporting to be the year the town was founded, is incorrect. The correct date is 1680, as the following information taken from the original records shows.

In June of 1680, Thomas, Lord Culpeper, the royal governor of Virginia, informed the Virginia Assembly at Jamestown that King Charles II, who had bestowed the name, "The Old Dominion" on Virginia because of its loyalty to the throne during the English Civil War, had commanded him to urge the establishment of towns in Virginia. Culpeper added that no nation had ever begun a colony without them and that no colony had ever prospered until they developed.

On the strength of this suggestion, the Assembly passed "An Act for Co-habitation and the Encouragement of Trade and Manufacture," providing that a town be established on a fifty-acre site in each of the twenty then existing counties. In specifying the various sites for these settlements, the act provided for a town "in Lower Norfolk County on Nicholas Wise his land on the Eastern Branch of the Elizabeth River at the entrance of the Branch."

The site chosen for "Norfolk Towne" was well-protected, having a fort at its western extremity which had been provided for by an act of the Assembly in 1673 and which had been built shortly thereafter. The site was also almost an island, being bounded on the west and south by the Elizabeth River and on the north and east by two creeks named Back Creek and Dun-in-the-Mire Creek, respectively. A narrow isthmus where City Hall Avenue and St. Paul's Boulevard now intersect then connected the proposed townsite with the country to the north of these two bodies of water.

On August 18, 1680, the justices of Lower Norfolk County,

acting on the strength of the act passed by the Virginia Assembly two months earlier, instructed the sheriff of the county to notify John Ferebee, the county surveyor, to begin the survey of the townsite on October 7, 1680. The justices also requested that all interested citizens be notified from the pulpits of the churches of the proposed establishment of the town, adding that anyone who cared to be present when the survey began was welcome.

By October 19, 1680, the survey had been made, and Ferebee was paid "for surveying the towne land and officiating as Cl(erk) of the Militia." Exactly one year later, on October 19, 1681, Ferebee received another payment "as Clerke of the Militia & laying out the Streets of the Towne."

These were Main Street; "the street that leadeth down to the waterside," later known as Market Square, the Parade, and Commercial Place; "the street that leadeth into the woods," later known as "the street that leadeth out of town" and still later as Church Sreet; "the street that leadeth to the publique spring," later known as Metcalf Lane; and a small right angle of a street north of the eastern end of Main Street that later became East Street and Bermuda Street.

In the meantime, word was received that King Charles II had changed his mind about establishing towns in Virginia and had suspended the 1680 act of the Virginia Assembly on December 21, 1681, on the advice of his Privy Council. But the Lower Norfolk County justices decided to go ahead with the project anyway. And on August 16, 1682, Lieutenant Colonel Anthony Lawson and Captain William Robinson, acting on behalf of the county court, bought the already surveyed townsite with its five clearly designated thoroughfares for ten thousand pounds of tobacco in cask from Nicholas Wise the younger, a shipwright, who had inherited the land from his father, Nicholas Wise the elder, who had owned it since 1662.

Besides handling the transfer of the fifty-acre site from Wise to the county, Lawson and Robinson were appointed feoffees by the court with the power to grant each half-acre lot in the purchased area to any person who would build a dwelling or warehouse thereon and settle on each lot so granted within three months, the price of each lot in the new town being one hundred pounds of tobacco.

Chapter Eight

Watching Norfolk's First Steps

The first recorded indication that Norfolk was beginning to develop as a port is preserved in the writings of the Reverend Francis Makemie (c.1658-1708), the founder of Presbyterianism in America. But it was Colonel William Byrd II of Westover (1674-1744) who set down the first known eyewitness description of the rapidly growing town.

Writing in 1705, twenty-five years after Norfolk had been established, Makemie said, "There are beginnings of towns at Williamsburg, Hampton and Norfolk, particularly at Norfolk-town at Elizabeth River, who carry on a small trade with the whole bay."

Byrd's more detailed description, written about thirty years later, comes from two related sources: "The Secret History of the Line," his day-to-day jottings when he was one of the Virginia commissioners to see that the boundary line between Virginia and North Carolina was properly surveyed, and his detailed narrative, written later from these notes, entitled "The History of the Dividing Line betwix Virginia and North Carolina Run in the Year of Our Lord 1728."

Byrd arrived in Norfolk on March 1, 1728, for a three-day stay, and was entertained that evening by Colonel George New-ton, then high sheriff of Norfolk County, later mayor of Norfolk in 1736 and 1742.

"Mrs. Newton provided a clean supper without any luxury about 8 o'clock," Byrd wrote in his Secret History, "and appeared to be one of the fine ladies of the town and, like a true fine lady, to have a great deal of contempt for her husband."

The next night, Byrd was invited "to an oyster and a bowl by Mr. Sam Smith, a plain man worth 20,000 Pounds. He produced his two nieces, whose charms were all invisible." In summing up the evening, Byrd added, "The parson and I returned to our quarters in good time and good order, but my man Tom broke the rules of hospitality by getting extremely drunk in a civil house."

In the meantime, between junkets, Byrd had been looking around, and this is how he described the Norfolk of 1728.

"Norfolk has more the air of a town of any in Virginia. There were then near twenty brigantines and sloops riding at the wharves, and oftentimes they have more. It has all the advantages of situation requisite for trade and navigation. . . . Their trade is chiefly to the West Indies, whither they export abundance of beef, pork, flour, and lumber. The worst of it is, they contribute much toward debauching the country by importing abundance of rum, which, like gin in Great Britain, breaks the constitutions, vitiates the morals, and ruins the industry of most of the poor people of this country. . . ."

In describing the town itself, Byrd wrote, "The town is built on a level spot of ground upon Elizabeth River, the banks whereof are neither so high as to make the landing of goods troublesome or so low as to be in danger of overflowing. The streets are straight and adorned with several good houses, which increase every day. It is not a town of ordinaries or public houses, like most others in this country, but the inhabitants consist of merchants, ship carpenters, and other useful artisans, with sailors enough to manage their navigation."

As a footnote, Byrd added, "With all these conveniences it lies under two great disadvantages that most of the towns in Holland do by having neither good air nor good water. The two cardinal virtues that make a place thrive, industry and frugality, are seen here in perfection; and so long as they can banish luxury and idleness the town will remain in a happy and flourishing condition."

Chapter Nine

Norfolk Becomes a Borough

Fifty-six years after its establishment as a town by an act of the Virginia Assembly in 1680, Norfolk was created a borough by royal charter on September 15, 1736. The charter was granted, and the letters of patent were witnessed by William Gooch, lieutenant governor and commander-in-chief of the Colony and Dominion of Virginia at Williamsburg, in the tenth year of the reign of King George II.

For its governing body, the charter specified that the borough should have "a mayor, one person learned in the law, styled and bearing the office of recorder of the said borough, eight aldermen, and sixteen other persons to be common councilmen."

Samuel Boush I, the "old Colonel Boush" who had "stirred his old bones very cheerfully in our service" when William Byrd II passed through Norfolk in 1728 on his way to act as a Virginia commissioner in the surveying of the boundary line between Virginia and North Carolina, was named in the charter as Norfolk's first mayor. As he died before November 18, 1736, however, the date of the first borough council meeting, George Newton was named mayor in his place.

Norfolk's first recorder, Sir John Randolph (1693-1737), one of the leading Virginians of his day and the only native Virginian to be knighted during the Colonial period, was also sworn in at the same meeting. Incidentally, it was the only one he ever attended, because he appointed Major David Osheal as his deputy immediately after his swearing in.

The eight men who became Norfolk's first aldermen in 1736 were typical of the solid citizens who were responsible for the town's pre-Revolutionary prosperity.

George Newton (1678-1762), Norfolk's first active mayor,

a son of an earlier George Newton, was educated in England. He was high sheriff and a justice of Norfolk County and a member of the Virginia Assembly at Williamsburg. He was mayor of the borough again in 1742.

Samuel Boush II, called "the younger," was a son of the man who had been named mayor in the borough charter. He was the first clerk of the Norfolk Borough Court.

John Hutchings (1691-1768), a son of Daniel Hutchings, a mariner, and a grandson of John Hutchings of "Pembroke Tribe" Bermuda, succeeded Newton as mayor and was again mayor in 1743 and 1755. He is buried near the south gate of St. Paul's Churchyard.

Robert Tucker II, the oldest son of Robert Tucker I, a wealthy Norfolk merchant who presented the still-preserved London wrought silver chalice and paten to the "Parish Church of Norfolk Towne" at the time of his death in 1722, succeeded Hutchings as mayor in 1738 and was again mayor in 1749 and 1759.

John Taylor (1694-1744), a native of the parish of Fintrie in the County of Sterling, Scotland, was mayor of Norfolk in 1739 and 1744. His handsome armoral tombstone in St. Paul's Churchyard was moved there several years ago from his private graveyard on the site of the present Customs House.

Samuel Smith, the younger, is a bit of an enigma, for when the elder Samuel Smith died in 1739, he referred to him in his will as "my friend Samuel Smith alias Samuel Coverley." In any event, the younger Samuel Smith presented the borough with its first known seal, a silver one with velum wafers, on June 24, 1740.

James Ivy (or Ivey) was also a vestryman of Elizabeth River Parish and a justice of the peace for Norfolk County. When he died in 1752, he saw to it that his widow would not be without firewood by leaving "Unto my loving Wife during her Widdowhood Liberty to Cutt Timber of the land I bought from Mr. John Taylor."

Of Alexander Campbell, little is known except that he was a merchant and owner of vessels and that Campbell's Wharf on the old Norfolk waterfront was named for him.

Chapter Ten

The Norfolk Mace

Norfolk's historic silver Mace, the only existing pre-Revolutionary American symbol of civic authority of its kind, has a long and interesting history.

Its presentation to the Borough of Norfolk in 1754 by Robert Dinwiddie (1693-1770), lieutenant governor of Virginia from 1751 to 1758, climaxed a friendship between the colonial official and Virginia's principal port of entry and exit dating back almost three decades.

Born in Glasgow, Scotland, Dinwiddie entered the colonial service at an early age and was collector of customs in Bermuda from 1727 to 1738. In the latter year he was promoted to surveyor general of the customs for the Southern ports of America, and as holder of the post he became a member of the Virginia Council in 1741.

As surveyor general of customs and council member, Dinwiddie became intimately acquainted with Norfolk's mercantile and civic affairs. And when the borough officials made him a burger, he reciprocated by presenting them with a seal, which was duly acknowledged at a meeting of the Norfolk Common Council on July 7, 1741.

Twelve years later, when Dinwiddie was lieutenant governor of Virginia, he again showed his appreciation by presenting the borough with the Mace.

Made in London of pure silver by Fuller White, the Mace

has an inscription stating it was given to the Corporation of Norfolk in 1753. It was not until the next year, however, that it was delivered, for the minutes of the Norfolk Common Council for April 1, 1754, explicitly state that Dinwiddie delivered the Mace in person and was gratefully thanked for the handsome gift.

According to tradition, the Mace was removed with the public records to Kempe's Landing (now Kempsville) at the time of the burning of Norfolk in January of 1776 and was returned only after the danger passed.

In its earlier days the Mace was always carried ahead of the mayor upon his entering court or before him in processions. On September 15, 1836, it was carried in the parade honoring the one hundredth anniversary of Norfolk as a borough, and on May 13, 1857, when the two hundred and fiftieth aniversary of the landing at Jamestown was observed, it was taken to Jamestown Island to be a part of the celebration.

In May of 1862, when Norfolk was evacuated by the Confederate forces, it was hidden by Mayor William Wilson Lamb under a hearth in his home on West Bute Street.

After the Civil War the Mace fell on evil days and was practically forgotten until 1894, when Norfolk Chief of Police C. J. Iredell discovered it in a state of disrepair in a heap of litter and old records in a room at the police station.

At that time, Norfolk city officials asked the Norfolk National Bank, now a part of the Virginia National Bank, to accept its custodianship. And in its carefully restored state it is displayed in a specially built glass case in the downtown Norfolk main office of the bank, where it is visited and admired annually by thousands of tourists and schoolchildren.

Chapter Eleven

Everyday Life in Pre-Revolutionary Norfolk

For those of a later generation with a yen to know what everyday life in pre-Revolutionary Norfolk was like, it was fortunate that an old citizen with a good memory dropped in for a leisurely chat with the editor of the Norfolk Herald in the 1830s.

The result of the conversation was a delightfully detailed article headed "Old Times" that appeared in the Herald of January 7, 1835, by far the best preserved account of the people and the customs of the borough of that era. In those days, the old man recalled, Norfolk was a "rare place indeed," its harbor being "filled with ships swallowing up cargoes of innumerable little schooners and sloops from adjoining rivers laden with tobacco, wheat, corn, lumber, etc."

Pre-Revolutionary Norfolk society, according to the same source, was divided into three distinct classes. The top of the ladder was reserved for the clergy, doctors, lawyers, merchants, and "those who lived on their incomes." The next rung down was occupied by the town's many skilled artisans, who were, however, "respected in their class." At the bottom were the "canaille" or "tag-rag and bobtail."

Architecturally, the old man remembered, the Norfolk of his youth was not a place of beauty. A few substantial brick buildings like the Borough Church of 1739, the Norfolk County Court House, and the Mason's Hall, where Norfolk's upper crust occasionally tripped the light fantastic to the accompaniment of fiddles amid dripping tallow or wax candles, were outstanding.

In the main, however, the unlighted and unpaved streets and lanes were lined with warehouses or Dutch or hip-roofed, dormer-windowed houses with a chimney at each end and a passage in the middle, dividing the dining room from the "hall or withdrawing room." But despite this drabness, that didn't mean that pre-Revolutionary Norfolk was dedicated to all work and no play. And at election times or on the occasion of the town's annual fair on October 3 and the four following days, a rip-roaring time was usually had by all.

The Parade or Market Square, later known as Commercial Place, was always the center of these affairs that were marked by all sorts of horseplay.

At election times, the old man recalled, hogsheads of punch and grog with their heads knocked out and abundant supplies of ginger cakes were provided by the "headmen" of the opposing parties for the refreshment of their followers, while all bets at those times were decided at a tavern over an "infant" of arrack punch and jelly, an "infant" being a large china bowl of a two-gallon capacity.

The old man also recalled the lusty sports that characterized the fair-time diversions of his youth. At those times a well-soaped and greased pole would be set up in the center of the square, on top of which a "gold laced hat" would be placed as a prize for the "lucky dog" who could shinny up its slippery height and bring it down. At other times four nimble-footed damsels would run a race for a fine chemise; pigs would be turned loose in the milling crowd to be claimed by anyone who could catch hold of them by their shaved, greased tails; sack races were run by men encased in burlap bags up to their necks; or four lusty, and possibly half-drunk, fellows would race through three empty sugar hogsheads that had been laced end to end, resulting in a rolling and tumbling that made the spectators yell with glee.

Also in those pre-Society for the Prevention of Cruelty to Animals days, a bull was frequently baited by a pack of fierce dogs, a dangerous sport that usually sent the spectators scampering to the rooftops for safety.

Chapter Twelve

A Colorful Pre-Revolutionary Mayor

It took a cool head and plenty of self-confidence to charge into a mob of brawling sailors and come out unscathed. Fortunately, Maximilian Calvert (1722-1782), Norfolk's most colorful pre-Revolutionary mayor, had both qualities in abundance. This is how his daughter, Mrs. Helen Calvert Maxwell Read, tells the anecdote in her memoirs:

"My father was for many years an alderman of the Borough Court and sometime Mayor of Norfolk. One night, it seems, there was a great riot in Portsmouth, from the sailors of a Spanish ship who had broken loose and taken the streets and were carrying all before them. The trustees and citizens came out to stop them, but without effect, when they bethought themselves to send over to the Mayor of Norfolk for help. My father, of course, repaired with all dispatch to the scene, dressed out in his best coat with his long cane, and a posse of gentlemen and constables in his train, and rushing into the midst of the mob, commanded them all to disperse in the name of the Commonwealth. This, however, though somewhat awed by his voice (which he had been used to raise in a gale of wind), they were rather unwilling to do, (and) demanded who he was that they should obey him. To which, aware of the respect which they all attached to long names, he dexterously replied, assuming his most dignified air, 'I am Don Maximilian Calverto, Grand Magistrate de Norfolco Boro'—upon which, not doubting he was a grandee of the first rank, they all took off their hats to him and returned very peacefully to their ship. This exploit, of course, got him great fame in those days."

Calvert, mayor of Norfolk in 1765 and 1769, was a picturesque character. He was the second of the thirteen children of Cornelius Calvert, the founder of a well-known old Norfolk family, and Mary Saunders Calvert, the daughter of an Anglican clergyman. He went to sea at an early age, and by the time he was in his late teens he was captain of a vessel sailing between

Norfolk and the West Indies, all of which made his daughter recall another good story concerning him.

"He had been ashore one day while his ship was lying in the harbor of Bridgetown to dine with a gentleman of that place, and returning on board rather late in the evening after having dined and drunk pretty freely, of course, as the fashion was, he found that the mate had turned in and fastened the cabin door, and unwilling to wake him up, he threw himself on the deck and slept the whole night.

"But the next morning he found that his knee was stiff, from the effect of the night air, and all the doctors whom he consulted were unable to restore it again. This defect, however, did not diminish but somewhat increased the stateliness of his gait, by making him carry himself still more erect, and his walk and carriage were imposing. He used to dress well, and wore the fine old-fashioned coat with large cuffs and ruffles at the hand. He was of gay and sociable disposition, fond of talking and joking, and lived on the best terms with his friends and neighbors."

Mayor Calvert also liked high living and this is how his daughter recalled his eating and drinking habits for posterity.

"My father was fond of good living, and kept a famous cook—poor old Quashabee, the ugliest creature my eyes ever beheld, but a capital cook, and made the best soups, sauces, gravies, and all such things, in the world. He was also fond of good drinking, though he never drank to excess. He was particularly fond of arrack punch (which, however, he drank weak), and always kept his silver tankard by him holding three pints, which he would empty two or three times a day, till the doctors began to be afraid he would fall into a lethargy, of which he showed some symptoms, and limited him to one."

Chapter Thirteen

Paul Loyall and the Press Gang

According to a breezy account preserved in The Virginia Gazette of October 1, 1767, press gangs attempting to recruit unwilling tars for the British Navy got a hot reception in pre-Revolutionary Norfolk.

Readers perusing that particular issue were treated to a full-column account of a press gang riot that had taken place in Norfolk one month earlier. The news was a trifle stale, for day-to-day reporting at that time was practically unheard of, but the event was still titillating.

Late on the night of September 5, 1767, Captain Jeremiah Morgan of His Majesty's sloop-of-war Hornet, anchored off Norfolk, embarked in his vessel's tender with several officers and thirty seamen, all armed to the teeth. The tender was rowed to the Public Wharf where it was made fast across the end so that its loaded swivel gun might command the wharf.

Going to a nearby tavern, they indulged in a "cheerful glass" or two and then proceeded to the lanes and alleys near the waterfront where they forced the boarding house keepers with curses and threats to open their doors. When the latter were led to believe that the party had a warrant from the mayor, they took down the bars. At that point the Britishers rushed in "like so many tigers and wolves" and began impressing seamen for the Hornet. And when several sailors put up a fight, they knocked them on their heads with stout oaken clubs and "lugged them away like dogs."

Raising the alarm by yelling, "A riot by man of war's men, with Captain Morgan at their head!" the Borough Watch caused the drums to be beaten, and this uproar brought the townspeople running into the streets.

Among them was Paul Loyall, a former mayor, who stood

six feet in his stocking feet. In his excitement, Loyall turned out clad only in his nightshirt and a pair of unbuckled shoes. Loyall's first gesture to restore law and order was to collar two British seamen who were dragging a protesting sailor off to the tender. And when the sailor managed to break loose from his captors, the Britishers were seized by the mob and dragged off to jail.

Loyall then headed a party of aroused citizens to where Captain Morgan and a party of armed sailors had fled near the Public Wharf. Demanding the reason why he had dared to disturb the peace at that time of the night, Morgan answered by swearing that he would run Loyall through with his sword. When Loyall reminded Morgan that he was unarmed, the half-drunk captain thrashed the air in the former mayor's direction with his sword.

Loyall stood his ground, however, and later remarked dryly, "If he (Loyall) had been an elephant of overgrown size, Morgan might have hit his head or his tail."

At that point, Mayor George Abyvon arrived with a posse of citizens. Making himself known, he commanded peace in the King's name, but Morgan "damned him and every man in Norfolk" and ordered his men to fire the swivel gun.

Fortunately, this did not happen, and the infuriated Morgan and a sailor leaped into a small boat and rowed hastily back to the Hornet, leaving the remainder of his party high and dry on the wharf at the mercy of the thoroughly aroused Norfolk citizenry.

By that time the shoe was on the other foot. The impressed seamen were freed and ten of the ringleaders of the press gang were put in jail. The rest of the Britishers were permitted to return to their ship.

Chapter Fourteen

George Washington in Norfolk

George Washington visited the Norfolk area many times, but according to historical evidence he was in Norfolk proper on only two occasions. The initial visit was on May 25, 1763, when the thirty-one-year-old Washington was on his way to visit the Dismal Swamp for the first time. The second was on May 28-29, 1763, when he was on his way back to Mount Vernon.

Washington first passed through the Norfolk area late in 1751, when he sailed with Lawrence Washington, his half brother, out of the Virginia Capes for the Barbadoes. After returning by the same route a few months later, he was absent from the Norfolk area until 1763, when he became interested in the Dismal Swamp as a money-making proposition.

Washington, along with five others, had formed a company known as "Adventurers for the Draining of the Great Dismal Swamp." The company had acquired about forty thousand acres of rich timberland in the swamp, and Washington, as manager of the company, visited the swamp to gain firsthand information about it.

Leaving Mount Vernon on May 16, 1763, Washington set out for Williamsburg to attend an extra session of the House of Burgesses. On Wednesday, May 25, 1763, according to his carefully kept expense accounts, he set out on horseback down the Virginia Peninsula for Hampton, where he paid one shilling, five pence to be ferried over to Norfolk. Arriving there, Washington took another ferry to Portsmouth, paying one shilling, six pence for his fare, and proceeded to Colonel Edward Riddick's plantation in Nansemond County, from which he set out to explore the Great Dismal, which he described as "a glorious paradise."

On Saturday, May 28, 1763, he arrived at Great Bridge in Norfolk County, from where he rode into Norfolk and stayed overnight at a tavern kept by John Reinsburg, paying him one pound, seventeen shillings, and six pence for board, lodging, and horse hire. Tradition says that since Washington was in Norfolk on a Sunday, he attended Morning Prayer at the Borough Church, now St. Paul's Episcopal Church. But there is no contemporary evidence that he did so.

After taking a ferry for Hampton on Sunday, May 29, Washington rode back to Mount Vernon by way of Williamsburg.

Washington is known to have made at least five other visits to his lands in the Dismal Swamp, but there is no record that he ever passed through Norfolk again. Records indicate that he used Suffolk as a base from then on because of its closer proximity to the swamp. But when Washington wanted his Dismal Swamp holdings charted, he entrusted the survey to Gershom Nimmo (? -1764), the surveyor of Norfolk County, whose map, dated "Norfolk, 20 November 1763," has been preserved. This chart includes the earliest known map of Lake Drummond.

Two other Norfolk-area Washington associations deserve mention.

On September 18, 1781, a month before the British troops under Lord Cornwallis laid down their arms at Yorktown while the bands played "The World Turned Upside Down," Washington, accompanied by members of his staff and several French officers, dined and held a council of war with Admiral Compte Francois Joseph Paul de Grasse aboard his flagship, the Ville de Paris, off Cape Henry. When the six-foot Washington came aboard and was hugged around the middle by De Grasse, a short, stocky man, and was addressed as "Mon petit general!" everyone laughed heartily, launching the conference on a merry note.

The other incident took place in Norfolk on February 22, 1800, two months after Washington's death On that occasion, thousands of Norfolk-area citizens, wearing deep mourning, marched to dirgelike music behind an empty black coffin to what is now St. Paul's Episcopal Church for a solemn funeral

service, minus the corpse, in memory of the recently departed
Father of His Country.

Chapter Fifteen

Streets Where History Walked

Despite the drastic face-lifting that downtown Norfolk
has undergone during the last few years, it still retains
enough of its pre-Revolutionary street names to link it with its
earliest history.

Of these, Main Street and Church Street (the lower part of
the latter now being known as St. Paul's Boulevard) are
the oldest.

Main Street, laid out between 1680 and 1681 by John Ferebee,
the Lower Norfolk County surveyor when the town was
established, extended from Four Farthing Point (later Town
Point) to Dun-in-the-Mire Creek (later Newton's Creek) in the
east. Its original zigzag shape, now considerably truncated,
followed the high ground between creek branches.

Church Street, first known as "the street that leadeth into
the woods" and later as "the street that leadeth out of town,"
originally crossed a natural causeway connecting the land on
which the town was first laid out and the country to the north of
Town Back Creek and Dun-in-the-Mire Creek. It was later called
Church Street because the Norfolk Borough Church, now St.
Paul's Episcopal Church, stood on its west side.

Norfolk's first notable real estate boom took place in the
early 1760s when Gershom Nimmo surveyed the extensive
property holdings of Samuel Boush III north of Town Back
Creek. It was at that time that many downtown Norfolk streets
received their present names. These are:

Boush Street, named for Samuel Boush III, the owner of
the land.

Granby Street, named for John Manners (1721-1770), Marquis of Granby, a popular military hero of the Seven Years War.

Cumberland Street, named for William Augustus, Duke of Cumberland (1721-1765), the uncle of George III who defeated Prince Charles Edward Stuart (the Young Pretender, popularly called Bonnie Prince Charlie) and his Jacobite forces at Culloden Moor, Scotland, in 1746.

Charlotte Street, named for Princess Charlotte Sophia of Mecklenburg-Strelitz, who married King George III in 1761.

Freemason Street, so called because the Norfolk Royal Exchange Lodge of Masons erected the "Mason's Hall" on a lot on the southeast corner of Freemason and Cumberland streets bought by them on July 11, 1764. The Willoughby-Baylor House now stands on that site.

Bute Street, named for John Stuart, Third Earl of Bute (1713-1792), a Scottish favorite of George III, and British prime minister from 1762 to 1763. He is principally remembered today because he granted Dr. Samuel Johnson, whom James Boswell immortalized in his famous biography, a pension of three hundred pounds a year.

Other old Norfolk streets that still retain their pre-Revolutionary names are Fenchurch, York, Duke, Yarmouth, Dunmore, and Botetourt streets, but the origins of their names, except for the last two, are obscure.

Dunmore Street was named for John Murray, Fourth Earl of Dunmore (1732-1809), governor of Virginia from 1771 to 1775. Dunmore began the destruction of pre-Revolutionary Norfolk on January 1, 1776, when his ships opened fire on the town.

Botetourt Street takes its name from Norborne Berkeley,

Baron de Botetourt (1718-1770), Colonial governor of Virginia from 1768 to 1770.

One other Norfolk thoroughfare bearing a corruption of its pre-Revolutionary name deserves mention. This is Magazine Lane, a few feet west of Granby Street, running north from Brambleton Avenue to Olney Road.

This lane, originally called Gunpowder Street, received its name because a powder magazine to contain ordnance for the defense of Norfolk was built there in 1774 in compliance with an act of the Virginia Assembly passed two years earlier.

Chapter Sixteen

The Borough Church

All Episcopal churches in Norfolk are directly descended from the first Anglican church of Elizabeth River Parish "at Mr. Seawell's Pointe," begun in the late 1630s and completed, according to the records of Lower Norfolk County, by March 15, 1640/41.

The church stood somewhere within the present western limits of the Norfolk Naval Station and continued in use for many years even though a "chapel of ease" was completed by 1641 farther down the Elizabeth River between Lamberts Point and what was later called Town Point in Norfolk. The chapel was erected for the convenience of the inhabitants of Lower Norfolk County who lived at a distance from the main church at Sewells Point.

Later, when Norfolk was laid out as a town in 1680-81, what is now St. Paul's Churchyard was set aside as a church site and burial ground. But no church was built there until after July 15, 1698, as a lot was granted on that date next to the present churchyard and there is no mention either of the church or the churchyard in the boundary designations.

Not more than a dozen families were living in Norfolk when it became the seat of Norfolk County in 1691, and those who did, no doubt, continued to use either the Sewells Point church or the "chapel of ease" nearer home. By 1693, however, the number of families in the town had practically doubled, and by 1698 there were at least thirty private establishments in Norfolk. The time had come, therefore, for the erection of a church within the town, which was begun probably late in 1698 and completed by 1700, when Samuel Boush I presented a still-preserved London-wrought silver chalice "to the Parish Church of Norfolk Towne March 1700."

The church was of brick and timber construction and stood near City Hall Avenue in the present churchyard. It remained in use until after 1739, when the present St. Paul's was built. And it was in this first church that Colonel William Byrd II of Westover and his companions worshiped on March 3, 1728, when they were on their way to assist in the surveying of the boundary line between Virginia and North Carolina.

Byrd's entry in his "Secret History of the Dividing Line" deserves quoting: "This being Sunday we were edify'd at Church by Mr. Marston with a good sermon. People could not attend their devotion for staring at us, just as if we had come from China or Japan."

The present church, the southeast gable of which is marked with the date 1739 and the letters "S.B." in raised bricks, was handsomely fitted up, befitting the increasing prosperity of Norfolk, which had been elevated to the distinction of a borough in 1736. The raised initials in the gable have always been presumed to be those of Samuel Boush I, a great benefactor of the church and Norfolk's first mayor, who had died in 1736, but there is no definite proof that this is so.

Be that as it may, the 1739 church, which received many handsome pieces of testimonial silver, several of which are still preserved, continued in use until the burning of Norfolk in January of 1776 by the British and Virginia forces, at which time its walls were among the few structures left standing in the borough.

After the Revolution, an act of the Virginia Assembly in October of 1785 permitted the holding of a lottery to re-roof the fire-gutted building. Later, after the first Christ Church was built in 1800 across Church Street from the old church that was then without a congregation, the building was used for a time as Norfolk's first Baptist church, a racially mixed one.

In 1832, however, the Rev. Henry W. Ducachet of Christ Church and his congregation were responsible for the rehabilitation of the old church, at which time it was renamed St. Paul's.

Chapter Seventeen

The Borough Churchyard

The tombstones of St. Paul's churchyard constitute an elegantly engraved stone directory of the Norfolk of the Eighteenth and early Nineteenth Centuries.

Although the churchyard was provided for when Norfolk was laid out in 1680-81, there are no original gravestones there remaining from that period, the three Seventeenth Century stones there having been brought from other places in Tidewater Virginia.

There are at present twenty-two pre-Revolutionary gravestones in the churchyard, although there no doubt were many more before deterioration destroyed them. The oldest is that of Mary Dyson, the wife of William Dyson, who died at the tender age of eighteen on January 3, 1748. The other pre-Revolutionary stones, many of them of English origin, some of them very beautiful examples of the stonecutter's art, memorialize the Archer, Taylor, Portlock, Hutchings, Rothery, Marsden, Tucker, and Calvert families, all of whom have left descendants or their mark on the topography of present-day Norfolk.

Almost every epitaph in St. Paul's churchyard is a novel

in miniature, but on none of them is this more evident than the inscription on the altar tomb of Mrs. David Duncan and her two children who died in 1823. The epitaph concludes with:

"Insatiate archer, could not one suffice?
Thy shaft flew thrice, and thrice my peace was slain."

Pathetic though this is, history records the cynical fact that the husband was not long without consolation, for the records of the Norfolk Corporation Court show that not quite a year after the death of his wife and children, he was again on the way to the altar.

Seven former mayors of Norfolk are buried in St. Paul's churchyard: John Tucker, Dr. John K. Read, Dr. James Taylor, Robert Taylor, John Hutchings, George Abyvon, and John Taylor, the elaborately carved armoral marker of the latter having been moved to its present place many years ago from the Taylor family cemetery in downtown Norfolk.

The churchyard that is a veritable museum of Eighteenth and early Nineteenth Century artistry in stone also contains the graves of two famous old Norfolk attorneys: General Thomas Mathews, for whom Mathews County was named, and Colonel John Nivison, who was remembered by Hugh Blair Grigsby, the Norfolk-born historian, this way:

"I can see this old man, too, with the freshness of the passing hour, as he was driving out in his capacious chariot to Lawson's or as he strolled or rather rocked (Col. Nivison weighed nearly 300 pounds) along the sidewalk. Whether he was fond of the classics, I cannot affirm; but he certainly borrowed a trait from Homer, and nodded occasionally, and when a tedious speaker began his harangue, having already taken a full view of the law and the facts in the case, he usually fell asleep, waking up as the counsel finished his harangue, much refreshed at least, if not instructed by it, and proceeded to give judgement in the case."

After having served the borough for about one hundred and forty-seven years, the old cemetery had become so crowded that an ordinance was passed denying burial to anyone whose near relatives had not already been buried there. And after the opening of Cedar Grove Cemetery, the city fathers put a stop to burials of all kinds there in 1835. Since then, interment there has required permission from the church vestry and a city ordinance.

Only seven people have made it so far: Mrs. Elizabeth Bacon in 1840; Mrs. Martha King, wife of former Norfolk Mayor Miles King, in 1849; Mrs. Rebecca Mann in 1851; Mrs. Mary Chandler, "Relict of George Chandler," in 1859; Dr. Nicholas Albertson Okeson, rector of the church for twenty-six years, in 1882; Dr. H. H. Covington, another rector, in 1933; and his wife in 1960.

Chapter Eighteen

The Ball in the Wall

If there is any doubt that the cannonball imbedded in the walls of Norfolk's historic St. Paul's Church is authentic, the following article should end it permanently. Signed "Native," the article appeared on Sunday, August 1, 1875, in The Norfolk Virginian. Headed "The Cannon Ball in Old St. Paul's," the piece has this to say:

"About the year 1848, the writer of this piece, then a pupil at Mr. Wm. R. Galt's school, held in the old Academy, Church Street, opposite St. Paul's Church, remembers seeing the old cannon ball immediately after it was found.

"It seems that the ball, fired from the British fleet, January 1, 1776, and which lodged in the south side of the head of the cross (the old church being constructed in the shape of a Latin cross), remained there for many years until, during the time the building was unused and the graveyard neglected, it fell from its position and was forgotten.

"Some years later the church was reopened by the present congregation, the building repaired and the cemetery put in order.

"About 1848 the assertion was made that the ball had fallen from its place unnoticed and was probably imbedded in the earth in the angle formed by the church and the street wall, and to test its correctness, the late Capt. F. W. Seabury, a vestryman of the church, got Mr. Wm. W. Lamb (also a vestryman) to send his servant with a spade to the churchyard.

"Under the direction of Capt. Seabury, the servant found the ball immediately under where it had first lodged in the wall, about 18 inches below the surface of the earth.

"The rusty old ball was seen soon after its resurrection by the writer, and was the identical one fired by the British frigate Liverpool into the venerable edifice.

"The same ball is now fastened in the wall with plaster, in the place it struck when fired."

So much for serious history. Now for two yarns concerning the cannonball from the anecdotal quiver of Armistead Bayne, director of Norfolk's MacArthur Memorial. Bayne, a former staff member of the Norfolk Redevelopment and Housing Authority, gleaned the two stories while acting as host to celebrities visiting the city.

This is how Bayne told them to James S. Walmsley, whose column, "At Large," has long been a popular feature in Commonwealth, The Magazine of Virginia.

"When Lord Louis Mountbatten visited Norfolk as First Lord of the Admiralty and one of NATO's chieftans, a group of Navy brass took him to see the cannonball. With some relish they pointed out that one of Lord Dunmore's warships fired the ball when the Royal governor was destroying Norfolk in one of the British Navy's less majestic episodes.

"After explaining what had happened, the Americans stood back and waited, perhaps with inward smirks, for the British sea dog's reaction. There was a long pause.

" 'Hahnnh,' Mountbatten snorted, gazing cooly at the projectile bulging from near the corner of the wall. 'Damn near missed it, didn't he?' "

Bayne's other cannonball yarn goes this way.

"Norfolk, as almost everyone knows, is a wonder of urban renewal. It is naturally proud of its achievement and often plays host to visiting urban renewal experts from other cities. One such group was being taken on a bus tour of the downtown with a Norfolk-trained urban renewal expert at the microphone explaining things. Glibly he rattled off a prodigious quantity of information without muffing a line or fact and then, with pride in the city's past, he pointed at the old church as they approached it and cried, 'And up on that wall gentlemen, is a cannonball fired by Cornwall Jackson!' "

Chapter Nineteen

The Dunmore Ball

It's a pity that the biggest social event of pre-Revolutionary Norfolk ended with a sour epilogue two years later. But considering the hectic temper of the times, it couldn't be helped.

The event was the ball given for John Murray, Fourth Earl of Dunmore, Virginia's last royal governor, and his countess in Norfolk in 1774. The epilogue was the bombardment of the town by Dunmore on January 1, 1776.

Dunmore had arrived in Virginia in the fall of 1771 and was joined early in 1774 by Lady Charlotte Dunmore and their children. A few months later the noble couple paid the still-loyal borough a visit, and an account of the event published in the Norfolk and Portsmouth Herald of July 3, 1818, and signed

"The Old Burgess," preserves much of the bouquet of the long past social event.

The affair was held in the Mason's Hall on Freemason Street, now the site of the Willoughby-Baylor House. Captain George Abyvon, the Norfolk mayor at that time, had some hesitancy when it came to dancing with Lady Dunmore, so an "express" was sent off to Princess Anne County for Colonel Edward Hack Moseley Jr. (1743-1814), "the finest gentleman we had, to come to town with his famous wig and shining buckles, to dance the minuet with my lady."

Needless to add "all the gentry of our town were there" together with "all the British navy officers . . . with their heads powdered as white as they could be." And when the fiddles struck up, Colonel Moseley led out Lady Dunmore "in her great, fine hoop-petticoat" for the first solo minuet, during which "little puss was too cunning for him" and "he was on the wrong scent more than once."

After that, Captain Abyvon was forced to take out Dunmore's daughter, Lady Catharine Murray, for another solo minuet. "But the poor Captain was laboring hard in a heavy sea all the time, and, I dare say, was glad enough when he got moored in his seat."

This was followed by still another minuet danced by Captain Montague of the Royal Navy and another Dunmore daughter, Lady Susan Murray, whom the old Norfolkian remembered forty-four years later as having made "a mighty pretty cheese with her hoop."

Once these formalities were cleared away, the party really got under way. And this is how "The Old Burgess" recalled what happened:

"Then came the reels; and here our Norfolk lads and lasses turned out with all their hearts and heels. This was my cue, and I led out my sweetheart, Nancy Wimble, in my best style, resolved to show all the sprigs of nobility what we Buckskins could do."

At that point, however, a young British officer became so smitten with Miss Wimble's charms that he took her away from her beau, "danced with her every time, and even managed to get her for the country dance, tho' I thought I had engaged her long before."

So Norfolk's most brilliant pre-Revolutionary social event ended on a wistful note as far as the young "Buckskin" was concerned. And this is how he philosophically summed it up:

"To say the truth, I believe the poor girl hardly knew what she did, she was so flattered and wheedled, and made a fool of by her red coat gallant. Indeed I soon found that she thought him worth two of me; and when she saw my Lady Dunmore call him to her, and tap him on the shoulder with her fan, it was really too much for her heart. In short, I was cut out, and cut down— and stole away from the ball with a flea in my ear. From this time, I saw plainly there was no chance for me. Indeed I could never get near her again; for the dashing officer was with her all weathers, and there was very little room between 'em, you see. Then she took to reading novels, and got a new hoop-petticoat to make her a Lady, and began to study what she could say when she came to stand before the King."

Chapter Twenty

The Press of a Patriot

Norfolk's first newspaper, the Virginia Gazette, or Norfolk Intelligencer, had a brief but memorable existance. Its first issue appeared on June 9, 1774, and what is believed to have been its last issue left the press on September 27, 1775.

The four-page weekly, the only known copies of which are preserved in the Library of Congress, was first published by William S. Duncan & Company, whose printing office was on the east side of the Parade or Market Square, later known as Commercial Place.

In April of 1775, John Hunter Holt became its publisher and the firm's name was changed to John H. Holt & Company. Holt, an ardent patriot and a son of John Holt, the public printer in Williamsburg, continued to issue the paper until it was suppressed late in September of 1775 by Lord Dunmore, the last royal governor of Virginia.

Because of mounting resistance to his arbitrary actions on the part of Virginia patriots, Dunmore had fled from Williamsburg in June of 1775 to the safety of the British warships in Norfolk-area waters. And as Norfolk had a large Tory element, he had made its harbor the base of his operations. This gave Holt his cue, and his paper began a steady, merciless needling of the unpopular governor.

Matters came to a head when Holt's paper of September 27, 1775, presumably contained several pointed reflections on the alleged treasonous actions on the part of Dunmore's father in the Jacobite Rebellion under Bonnie Prince Charlie in 1745. This and other taunts spurred Dunmore into action. And at noon on Saturday, September 30, 1775, he sent an officer and a detachment of British sailors and soldiers ashore to "the dirty little Borough of Norfolk" to confiscate Holt's press and printing materials and to capture Holt if possible.

Meeting no resistance, the landing party marched to the printing shop and seized Holt's "press, tipes, paper, ink, two of the printers, and all of the utensils." Holt's bookbinder, a man named Cumming, was also taken prisoner, but Holt, who according to one account of the fracas was hiding in the building, was not captured.

The raid was witnessed by several hundred persons, but apparently no one seemed inclined to do anything about the high-handed action. And after the landing party, with its loot and prisoners, returned to its boats, the onlookers were "joined by a crowd of negroes" in three loud huzzas.

The account containing this comment, dated Norfolk, September 30, 1775, continues: "A few spirited gentlemen in

Norfolk, justly incensed at so flagrant a breach of good order and the Constitution, and highly resenting the conduct of Lord Dunmore and the navy gentry, who have now commenced downright pirates and banditti, ordered the drum to beat to arms, but were joined by few or none; so that it appears Norfolk is at present a very insecure place for the life or property of any individual, and is consequently deserted daily by numbers of the inhabitants, with their effects."

Immediately after the raid, Norfolk Mayor Paul Loyall protested that it was "illegal and riotous," but Dunmore, who had watched the incident through a spyglass from one of his ships, arrogantly told Loyall that he had done Norfolk a favor by "scotching the printed viper that was pouring its poison in their midst."

Dunmore's seizure of Holt's press caused a hue and cry, and the Williamsburg papers stepped up their campaign against him, even alleging that he had "dared offer violence to the chastity of a poor innocent girl" from the Norfolk Poor House and had also kept a mistress while he was in Williamsburg. But that didn't effect the return of Holt's press, which was used by Dunmore to print a short-lived paper of his own aboard one of his ships.

Holt retaliated by announcing that he would set up another press in Norfolk, but this was prevented by the burning of the borough a few months later. Holt then joined the Revolutionary Army, and after Yorktown he was associated with John Dixon in publishing the Richmond Virginia Gazette and Independent Chronicle. He died in 1787.

Chapter Twenty-one

Methodism in Early Norfolk

The Reverend Robert Williams, a native of England, was the first Methodist to preach in Norfolk.

According to "The Beginnings of American Methodism" by John O. Gross (1961), Williams, who had been proclaiming the Gospel along the highways and byways of Ireland, resolved to be the first itinerant Methodist preacher to arrive in the British colonies.

Before setting out, Williams sold his horse to pay his debts. Since he did not have the money to pay for his passage, he set out for the port carrying his saddlebags on his arm. There an Irish friend paid for his passage, and he sailed for America.

William Warren Sweet in his "Virginia Methodism: A History" (1955) gives two versions of how Williams arrived in Norfolk.

The first account says he arrived from England on a Baltimore-bound ship in 1769. After leaving the vessel he proceeded up Main Stret with his Bible and hymnbook in his pockets until he came to a house that was advertised for rent.

Taking up his stand on the steps, he began to sing and soon attracted a motley crowd. Telling of his purpose in coming to America, he asked if anyone would give him a night's lodging.

At that point, a woman, whose ship-captain husband was away at sea, invited Williams to come home with her, whereupon Williams repaid her hospitality by converting her to Methodism.

The account ends on a strange note of extrasensory perception. The woman's conversion was revealed to her husband by some mystical process, and he duly entered what was revealed to him in the ship's log, only to have it corroborated when he returned home.

The second account states that Williams first came to Norfolk in 1772, and a contemporary observation jotted down by a Norfolkian of that time added that Williams "mounted the highest steps of the courthouse (the Norfolk County Court House at the head of Market Square) and commenced singing 'Come Sinners to the Gospel Feast' and I looked out at the door and said to my shop mates there is a crazy fellow at the courthouse and I will go and see him."

Williams did not receive a very cordial welcome in Norfolk because his hearers felt that his sermons contained too much hellfire and damnation. As a result, he moved his activities to Portsmouth, where he established a Wesley Society that eventually grew into the Monumental United Methodist Church of today.

Williams was followed in the Norfolk area by the Rev. Joseph Pilmoor, another Englishman, who is credited by historians for actually establishing the Methodist Church in Norfolk. Pilmoor recorded that when he was passing through Portsmouth on his way to Norfolk he came upon two men at the ferry who were "swearing most horribly."

"If I had been brought to this place blindfolded," he wrote, "I should have known I was near Norfolk."

Despite its initial setbacks, Methodism in Norfolk eventually took root and by 1775, when the Reverend Francis Asbury visited the borough, he found the Norfolk Methodists were worshiping in "an old, shattered building which had formerly been a playhouse."

The destruction of Norfolk during the Revolutionary War scattered the Norfolk Methodists for a while, but by 1793 they had established their first regular church on Fenchurch Street. Since the ground in that area was marshy, the church was built upon blocks eight feet high to protect it from being flooded by the high tides.

This church served the Norfolk Methodist congregation until February 1800, when a lot was purchased on Cumberland Street on a site now occupied by a parking lot for Old St. Paul's Episcopal Church.

The first brick church erected on this property in 1802, known as the Cumberland Street Methodist Church, was the mother church of all the Methodist congregations in Norfolk today.

Chapter Twenty-two

The Burning of Norfolk

When Miss Ann Archdeacon and her fiance, James Nimmo, applied for a marriage license on August 24, 1797, John Ingram, her guardian, wrote the following to the clerk of the Norfolk Corporation Court: "Miss Nancy Archdeacon was born on the first day of January 1776, a remarkable day for this town."

He was referring to the destruction of Norfolk by the British and colonial troops that began on New Year's Day of 1776. When it was completed, Norfolk had the dubious distinction of being the most devastated community of its size in the American colonies during the Revolution.

The Norfolk area, where the Tory element was strong, had been the base of operation for Lord Dunmore, the last royal governor of Virginia, since he had fled to the safety of the British warships in Virginia waters in June of 1775. And until his forces were defeated at the Battle of Great Bridge on December 9, 1775, he more or less had things under his control. Dunmore's defeat at Great Bridge, however, turned the tide and from then on Norfolk's fate hung in the balance.

Five days after the battle, the Virginia troops under Colonel William Woodford occupied the borough, from which most of the inhabitants, including the leading Tory families, had fled, the latter seeking refuge aboard Dunmore's already crowded ships in the harbor. Five days later, Colonel Robert Howe and his North Carolina provincial troops arrived, after which Howe assumed control of all of the colonial forces in Norfolk.

From then on, Howe's sharpshooters, stationed in high and secluded places along the waterfront, began picking off anyone who dared to show his head above deck on the British ships.

Intense cold, the crowded conditions aboard the ships, and near starvation finally forced Dunmore to act, but when he demanded food from Howe he flatly refused. This sparked the cannonading by the British that began the destruction of pre-Revolutionary Norfolk.

The firing began about 3:15 p.m. on New Year's Day of 1776, and continued until 2 a.m. on January 2. Under the cover of a constant bombardment of double-headed bar, chain, and grape-shot, British landing parties attempted to rifle the waterfront warehouses, but in most instances they were repulsed by Howe's men.

But Dunmore and his followers, popular tradition to the contrary, were not the only villains in the destruction of Norfolk. For according to H. J. Eckenrode's "The Revolution in Virginia" (1916), an authoritative source book on the subject compiled from original documents in the Virginia State Archives:

"The fires begun by balls and landing-parties, spread with great rapidity, because the provincial soldiers, instead of attempting to extinguish them, seized the opportunity to plunder and destroy on their own behalf, determined, as they said, 'to make hay while the sun shines.' Breaking into rum-shops and warehouses, many of them soon became drunk and went in gangs from house to house, smashing in doors, dragging out spoils, and then applying the torch. Household goods of every kind were sold in the streets for a song to anybody willing to buy. The destruction caused by the ships was confined to the waterfront, but the Virginia soldiers involved the whole place in the catastrophe. On January 2, 1776, when the firing had ceased, the riflemen continued their work of rapine without interference on the part of their officers—apparently even with their connivance. Only on the third day did Woodford put an end to the sack by forbidding the burning of houses under severe penalty, but by that time more than two-thirds of Norfolk was in ashes. In February, 1776, the remainder was destroyed by order of the convention in order to deprive Dunmore of shelter."

Chapter Twenty-three

The Coming of the French

Norfolk's population was principally of English, Scotch, and Irish origins until after the Revolutionary War. But with the coming of the French refugees from the slave uprising in Santo Domingo in 1793, the borough became more cosmopolitan.

Discovered by Columbus in 1492 and originally called Espanola, the island, now the Republic of Haiti, was ceded by the Spanish to the French in 1677. It was rapidly colonized by its new owners, and a highly profitable sugar plantation economy, worked by thousands of Negro slaves was developed.

Most of the slaves, many of whom had been born in Africa, outnumbered all of the other inhabitants of the island ten to one at the time of the outbreak of the French Revolution.

Taking advantage of long-standing differences between their white masters and the mulatto population of the island brought to a head by the unsettled state of affairs in the mother country, the long-restless slaves revolted. And in a few short months the once prosperous French West Indian colony was devastated by savage fighting.

Seeking revenge as well as freedom, the revolting blacks raped, tortured, and killed their former owners and any slaves who remained faithful to them and pillaged and destroyed their property.

News of the horrors that were being perpetrated in Santo Domingo continued to filter into Norfolk by way of incoming ships throughout the early 1790s. And in July of 1793, the problem became an acutely local one when a fleet of one hundred and thirty-seven square-rigged vessels loaded to the gunwales with half-starved refugees under the escort of two French ships of the line, three frigates, and three smaller warships sailed into Hampton Roads from Cape Francois (now Cape Haitien) that had been looted and burned by the rampaging slaves.

Although most of the vessels proceeded to Baltimore, many of them sailed up the Elizabeth River to Norfolk, and the borough was suddenly faced with the first out-of-all-proportion relief program in its history.

Writing to the Governor of Virginia on July 6, 1793, Thomas Newton Jr. of Norfolk had this to say concerning the pitiful condition of those on board the ships from Cape Francois:

"Husbands and wives, parents & children are distributed in such a manner that they Know not where to find each other . . . many were taken out of the water & thrown on board the vessels without cloathes or any subsistance whatever."

Three days later in another letter, Newton informed the governor that "20 odd sail" of the flotilla had docked in Norfolk, and "our place is crowded with Frenchmen, and too many Negroes have been brought in with them."

Coming to the assistance of the refugees, the State of Virginia voted a two-thousand-dollar grant, while subscriptions from private sources poured in, not only from Norfolk but also from almost every other town in Virginia.

According to Isaac Weld, the author of "Travels Through North America," who visited Norfolk in 1795, there were between two thousand and three thousand French in Norfolk at one time. But this number was greatly lessened later when many of the refugees either returned to France or moved to other parts of the United States.

Those who remained—and there were a great many, as shown by Simmons's 1801 and 1806-07 Norfolk Directories, the late Eighteenth and early Nineteenth Century marriage records of the borough, and tombstones in local cemeteries—became the ancestors of many Norfolk families of today.

Chapter Twenty-four

Music in Old Norfolk

Norfolk's earliest musical activities were principally of amateur nature with occasional performances by travelling professionals to relieve the monotony.

That there were persons in pre-Revolutionary Norfolk who could scrape a tune on a "fiddle" is well known. And it was these unknown musical tyros, many of them fiddle-playing slaves, who provided the music for the more elaborate balls at the Mason's Hall or for the more informal dances at weddings, christenings, and other festivities in the homes of the more wealthy.

It is also a matter of record that the more popular ballad operas of the period, such as "The Beggar's Opera," were performed by travelling companies on the stage of Norfolk's first theater on King's Lane, while the church music of that era was restricted to the singing of metrical versions of the Psalms, the only kind of music then heard in Virginia's Anglican churches.

After the Revolution, however, when Norfolk became more cosmopolitan and the visits of professional actors and musicians became more frequent, the musical horizons of the borough broadened considerably.

According to Simmons's Norfolk directories for 1801 and 1806-7, all of the Norfolk music masters of that period were either French or German. Later, in 1818, another musician, J. H. Hoffman, advertised in the Norfolk Herald for pupils, offering to teach the "clarionet, trumpet, French horn, bugle horn, oboe, grand hautboy or voce umane, trombone, fife, German flute or additional keyed flute, flageolet, Sacbut, viel hurdy or beggars lyre, violin, violoncello, bass viol, bass drum, cymbals, etc.," an amazing offer in any period.

Norfolk's first pipe organ was installed in the first Christ Church, built in 1800 on Church Street across from the old Borough Church. Its organist, James H. Swindells, Norfolk's first recorded "minister of music" was responsible for greatly improving the quality of church music in the borough.

On May 21, 1818, Swindells, directing a large group of singers and a "band composed of several eminent professors and a number of amateurs, among which were gentlemen of cultivated taste and fine power of execution," gave an appreciative audience of over a thousand its first taste of the music of Handel, Pergolesi, and other first-rate composers.

Forty years later, on August 31, 1858, Professor Philip H. Masi, Norfolk's leading musician of his time, led a picked group of soloists and singers in the city's first rendition of Rossini's "Stabat Mater" in the recently completed St. Mary's Catholic Church at Holt and Chapel streets.

Meanwhile, serious Norfolk music lovers were increasingly receiving more generous doses of professionally performed music. Travelling opera companies, featuring better than average performances of the then standard repertoire, appeared with relative frequency at the Church Street Opera House, which opened in 1856. On its stage early in April of 1864, Louis Moreau Gottschalk, America's first internationally known pianist and matinee idol, whose celebrated "bedroom eyes" kept his female auditors in a constant state of flutter, performed "several of his latest compositions that have caused such a sensation in Boston, Philadelphia, New York, and other cities."

Professional musicians visiting Norfolk at that time also appeared at the Mechanic's Hall on Main Street, completed in 1850, that finally ended its career as the Gaiety Theater, a burlesque house, in 1960.

On January 26, 1853, the ten-year-old Adelina Patti, who was to become one of the greatest coloratura sopranos of all time, appeared there in a joint recital with the Swedish violinist, Ole Bull, and thrilled Norfolk music lovers with her already phenomenal vocal pyrotechnics.

Chapter Twenty-five

Norfolk Theater History—Part I

Norfolk's recorded theatrical history dates from November 17, 1751, when a company of strolling actors headed by Walter Murray and Thomas Kean presented "The Recruiting Officer," a comedy by the Irish playwright, George Farquhar, in "Capt. Newton's Great Room."

From then until the Revolution, Norfolk, as Virginia's most important port, had a fairly active theatrical history.

Norfolk's first regular theater, however, was "a wooden structure that had originally been built as a pottery."

According to the reminiscences of an octogenarian published in the Norfolk Herald of June 19, 1839, this pottery, refurbished as a playhouse, "stood on the rear of a lot on the south side of Main Street, somewhere about King's Lane on the river margin."

It was in this building that the theatrical troupes that visited pre-Revolutionary Norfolk put on their performances, and it was also within its walls that a serious riot took place when the reminiscing octogenarian was a boy. This is how the Herald reported it:

"Norfolk in those days was pretty much of a John Bull sort of town, and a theatre row could be got up as summarily here as within the walls of the Old Drury or the Haymarket. One night when the tragedy of Theodosius, or the Force of Love, was to be played, our friend paid his half crown for a children's ticket and squeezed in amongst the crowd that filled the house to overflowing. The hour for the curtain to rise had passed and the audience began to testify their impatience in the usual way of stamping, thumping with sticks and umbrellas, whistling, etc., to which no response was made by the prompter's bell. A half hour passed beyond the time, and still there was no shew of beginning. Presently a nose and one eye, reconnoitering the audience through a hole in the green curtain, caught the attention of Lawyer Curle, who flung a bottle at the two inquisitive organs with such remarkable precision that their owner received the missive full in the forehead, and honored (it) by immediate prostration. This was a signal for a general row: the stage was invaded in a twinkling, the curtain torn down, and the scenery, including the sacred altar prepared for the first scene, shared the same fate."

Incidentally, the "Lawyer Curle" who was such a good marksman with a bottle was William Roscoe Wilson Curle, a member of a prominent Elizabeth City County family and a secretary of the Norfolk Sons of Liberty when that group was organized on March 31, 1766, to protest the Stamp Act.

Almost on the eve of the Revolution, the old King's Lane playhouse was used for another purpose, a meeting place for the Methodists of the borough.

According to Bennett's "Memorials of the Methodists in Virginia," when the Reverend Francis Asbury, the Anglo-American preacher and first bishop of the Methodist Episcopal Church in the United States, came to Norfolk in 1775, he found the persons of his sect meeting in an "old, shattered building which had formerly been a playhouse."

Here, according to the same source, the Reverend Mr. Asbury preached for the first time in Norfolk, to a congregation of one hundred and fifty persons.

A few months later, Norfolk's first Temple of the Muses went up in flames when Lord Dunmore, the last royal governor of Virginia, and the Virginia forces burned pre-Revolutionary Norfolk to the ground.

Chapter Twenty-six

Norfolk Theater History—Part II

Although theatrical performances were given fairly frequently in pre-Revolutionary Norfolk in "Capt. Newton's Great Room" and in Norfolk's first known theater, a converted pottery on King's Lane near the Elizabeth River, it was not until after the Revolution that the borough's theatrical life became really active.

As early as 1790, Norfolkians were flocking to see "The Irish Widow" and "The School for Scandal." But there was no regular playhouse in Norfolk until 1793, when a former warehouse on Calvert's Lane was used for that purpose.

This makeshift theater was operated by Thomas Wade West and John Bignall, two well-known American actor impresarios of their day who were also responsible for the erection of Norfolk's first regular theater in 1795 on property that had been purchased by them on July 12, 1792.

The building was of brick and stood midway of the block on the east side of Fenchurch Street between East Main and Bermuda streets. On its stage, David and Elizabeth Arnold Poe, the parents of Edgar Allan Poe, acted for several seasons; John Howard Payne, the author of "Home Sweet Home," played "Hamlet" and other tragic roles as a youth; and Junius Brutus Booth, the father of John Wilkes Booth, Lincoln's assassin, appeared in Shakespeare's "Richard III" and other melodramatic roles in November of 1821.

Two years later the building was sold to the Methodist Protestant congregation and on March 6, 1845, it was destroyed by fire.

Norfolk was without a regular theater until 1839, when the Avon Theater was built. It stood on the site of the former Norfolk police headquarters, just behind the present MacArthur Memorial, and was an elegant building with an impressive portico supported by six massive Doric columns, with a bust of Shakespeare in its pediment. It burned in February of 1850.

Norfolk's next theater was the Mechanic's Hall on the south side of Main Street, a "Tudor Gothic" building that was frst opened in 1850. It was used for years as a recital hall by travelling musicians and also as a place for political rallies. It ended its career as the Gaiety Theater, a burlesque house, and was torn down in 1960.

The Norfolk Varieties or Church Street Opera House was next. It was opened in 1856, and stood on the west side of Church Street between the present Plume Street and City Hall Avenue. The finest actors and singers of their day appeared on its stage during its long career, but there were times when the performances were not up to par. For instance, in reviewing a travelling opera company in 1865, a Norfolk newspaper critic wrote:

"Such demoniac howlings were never heard outside of Pluto's dreary kingdom, and we can only compare the entire performance to a midsummer night when all the dogs and cats are loose."

The Church Street Opera House held its own until 1880, when the Academy of Music, the finest theater in the South at that time, was erected on Main Street on the present site of the south entrance of the Selden Arcade.

The Academy was the most elegant theater ever erected in Norfolk. Its great electrically lighted chandelier, the first of its kind in the city, that hung from an elaborately frescoed ceiling in which medallion portraits of Shakespeare, Racine, Beethoven, Goethe, Mozart, Haydn, Schiller and Mendelssohn were inserted, was one of the major attractions of the Norfolk of its era.

Its spacious stage was also the glittering showcase for every great actor, concert artist, vocal artist and opera company that visited Norfolk for almost half a century.

Finally, on April 4, 1930, the Academy, that had been degraded to a cheap movie house, after which it was boarded up during the Great Depression for lack of patrons, was destroyed by fire.

Chapter Twenty-seven

Norfolk's Presbyterian Beginnings

Although the Anglican Church was the only officially recognized religion in Virginia until its disestablishment by an act of the Virginia Assembly in December of 1776, it is a matter of record that there were Presbyterians in the Norfolk area as early as the second half of the Seventeenth Century. Because of restrictions placed on dissenters by the civil authorities, however, Norfolk area Presbyterians had no regular churches, and what meetings that were held took place in private homes with the grudging approval of the county court.

Pre-Revolutionary Norfolk Presbyterian history, despite the large number of prosperous Scots who lived in the borough, is not too well documented. But it is known that the Reverend Francis Makemie (c.1658-1708), regarded as the chief founder of the Presbyterian Church in America, administered to the Presbyterians on "Elizabeth River in Virginia" off and on from 1684 to 1692.

Upon his arrival in the Norfolk area, he wrote: "I found there a poor, desolate people mourning the loss of their dissenting minister from Ireland whom the Lord had pleased to remove by death the previous summer."

Makemie, who was later described by Lord Cornbury, the royal governor of New York, as a "Jack of all Trades; he is a Preacher, a Doctor, a Merchant, an Attorney or Counsellor at Law, and what is worse of all, a Disturber of Governments," was succeeded in the Norfolk area by the Reverend Josias Mackie, an Anglican clergyman with Presbyterian leanings, who died in 1716. From then on, Norfolk Presbyterian history is vague

PLATE I. *The Princess Elizabeth Stuart (1596-1660), daughter of James I of England. The Elizabeth River, Norfolk's main waterway, was named for her. The portrait, dated 1612, was painted when she was sixteen. From the collection of George Spencer Churchill at Northwick Park, Gloucestershire, England.*

PLATE II. *This British cannonball imbedded in the walls of Norfolk's historic 1739 Borough Church, now St. Paul's Episcopal Church, was fired from one of Lord Dunmore's ships in the Elizabeth River on January 1, 1776, in the bombardment that began the destruction of pre-Revolutionary Norfolk.*

PLATE III. An early Nineteenth Century drawing of the Norfolk Borough Court House, erected in 1790-91 on East Main Street. It was used until May 20, 1850, when the Norfolk Court House and City Hall (now the MacArthur Memorial) was first used.

PLATE IV. *Late Eighteenth and Early Nineteenth Century Norfolk recognition flags painted on the sides of a Liverpool pitcher in the possession of Barton Myers III of Toronto, Canada. The colors of the buntings used in the original flags are indicated in the drawing. (See page 56).*

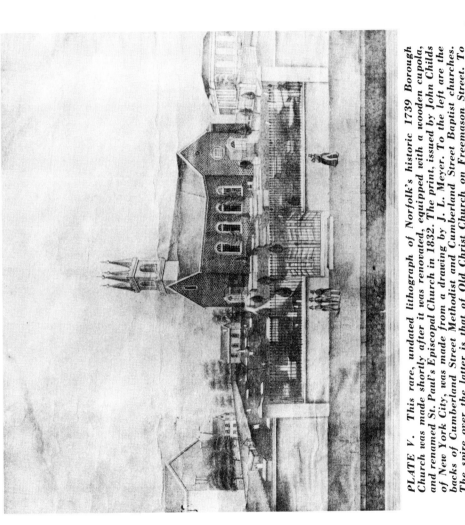

PLATE V. This rare, undated lithograph of Norfolk's historic 1739 Borough Church was made shortly after it was renovated, equipped with a wooden cupola, and renamed St. Paul's Episcopal Church in 1832. The print, issued by John Childs of New York City, was made from a drawing by J. L. Meyer. To the left are the backs of Cumberland Street Methodist and Cumberland Street Baptist churches. The spire over the latter is that of Old Christ Church on Freemason Street. To the right, behind the altar end of St. Paul's is Norfolk's second Presbyterian church on Church Street.

PLATE VI. *General Robert Barraud Taylor (1774-1834), commander of the American forces in the Norfolk area during the War of 1812, later the first judge of the Superior Court of Law and Chancery for the Borough of Norfolk.*

PRESBYTERIAN CHURCH. NORFOLK, 1802.

PLATE VII. Norfolk's first Presbyterian Church, at the northwest corner of Catharine (now Bank) and Charlotte streets. Completed in 1802, its belfry contained Norfolk's first known church bell, giving the edifice the name "The Bell Church."

PLATE VIII. *Market Square, later Commercial Place, in Norfolk in 1865. The print, a wood engraving after a drawing by James E. Taylor, is from the German edition of Frank Leslie's Weekly and is a delightful depiction of the Norfolkians of that period.*

PLATE IX. *The Old Norfolk Academy on Bank Street, begun in 1840 and opened in 1841. The building was designed by Thomas U. Walter of Philadelphia (1804-1887), one of the foremost architects of his period. From an old photo dating from around 1890.*

PLATE X. *The Norfolk Varieties or Church Street Opera House,*
opened in 1856. The building stood on the west side of Church
Street (now St. Paul's Boulevard), on the site later occupied by
L. Snyder's department store.

PLATE XI. Mrs. Col. Walter Herron Taylor of Norfolk (nee
Elizabeth Selden Saunders). From a photograph taken late in
her life. As a young lady, she was the first person to tell President
Jefferson Davis that Richmond was about to be evacuated. (See
story on page 97).

**PLATE XII. St. Mary of the Immaculate Conception, Norfolk's
oldest Catholic church, consecrated in 1858. It was called "the
best ante-bellum Gothic workmanship in the South" by Ralph
Adams Cram, the famous American architect and medievalist.**

PLATE XIII. *General Robert E. Lee, from a photograph presented to Miss Caroline Selden of Norfolk in April 1870, when he was a guest of her father, Dr. William Selden. From the original in the possession of C. Wiley Grandy of Norfolk.*

POST OFFICE—Norfolk.

PLATE XIV. *A late Nineteenth Century photograph of the United States Customs House and Post Office on Main Street, designed by Ami B. Young (1798-1874), a government architect. The building was begun in 1852 and completed in 1859.*

CHRIST CHURCH. Norfolk.

PLATE XV. An original watercolor drawing of Old Christ Church at Freemason and Cumberland streets, belonging to Christ and St. Luke's Episcopal Church, Norfolk. It is inscribed "Designed and Painted by T. Williamston 1828." The artist, Thomas Williamson, an amateur architect, designed the church. The small classical building in the lower center of the drawing was the Norfolk Athenaeum, erected in 1827 and destroyed by fire in 1859.

YORKTOWN CENTENNIAL, MAIN-STREET ARCH.

PLATE XVI. *The Yorktown Centennial Arch at Bank and Main streets, erected to commemorate the hundredth anniversary of the Battle of Yorktown. The old print shows the band leading the parade that highlighted a week-long celebration of the event in Norfolk during October 1881.*

until after the enactment of Thomas Jefferson's "Statute for Religious Freedom" by the Virginia General Assembly of 1784-85.

Free at last to establish a church of their own, a group of twenty-five Norfolk Presbyterians, most of them of Scottish birth, met on April 25, 1800, in the Norfolk Borough Court House and made plans to build a church on property bought for that purpose on the northwest corner of Charlotte and Catharine, (later Bank) streets. A subscription was opened at one hundred dollars a share to provide funds to build the church. Of the eighty-seven subscribers, the majority were of Scottish origin, but the enterprise was so popular that Moses Myers, one of Norfolk's merchant princes and a Sephardic Jew, was one of the shareholders.

As early as 1793, the Reverend Benjamin Porter Grigsby, who was to be the church's first minister, had been sent by the Presbyterian General Assembly in Philadelphia "to itinerate through the lower parts of Virginia" to administer to Presbyterians living there. Grigsby was so popular in Norfolk that he was invited to be the first minister of the new church, which was completed early in 1802, a few months after he had become its minister in 1801. Built of brick, the church was topped by a small, graceful cupola in which hung Norfolk's first known church bell, which gave the edifice its nickname "The Bell Church."

Grigsby married Elizabeth McPherson, a wealthy Norfolk girl, on January 2, 1806. Commenting on the marriage a sharp-tongued English lady then living in Norfolk wrote:

"He provident as pastors are,
  Soon turned his eyes among the fair;
  And singled out a girl with land,
  Negroes and money, at command;
(Thus striving hard, a case most common,
  To serve at once both God and mammon.)"

Be that as it may, the union produced Hugh Blair Grigsby (1806-1881), the celebrated Norfolk-born Virginia historian.

Four years later, the Reverend Mr. Grigsby was summoned one Sunday afternoon to conduct the funeral of a sailor who had died of yellow fever, and one week later he died of the same disease. He is buried in Trinity Churchyard in Portsmouth.

It is from "The Bell Church" that all of the Presbyterian churches in Norfolk descend.

Chapter Twenty-eight

Flags of Fortune

The painted recognition flags on the sides of a fragile Liverpool pitcher, now owned by Barton Myers III of Toronto, Canada, preserve one of the most interesting records of Norfolk's late Eighteenth and early Nineteenth Century commercial prosperity.

Recognition flags were oblong or pennant-shaped pieces of bunting on which the color code or the symbol of the merchant who owned the vessel were displayed. Since the pitcher bears the initials "T.W.," and since Thomas Willock's bunting is among those depicted, it is reasonable to assume that it originally belonged to him. Somewhere along the line, however, the pitcher came into the possession of Moses Myers, another prominent Norfolk merchant of that era. And its present owner is one of his direct descendants.

The pitcher dates from the late Eighteenth or early Nineteenth Century period when Norfolk enjoyed a span of tremendous commercial prosperity. With the signing of the Treaty of Paris in 1783, ending the Revolutionary War, foreign merchantmen began to enter the Capes again. And it was not long before Norfolk resumed its place as the chief port of entry and export for Virginia.

All of those whose flags and names appear on the pitcher amassed large fortunes from brisk trade with the West Indies during the Napoleonic Wars. And almost all of them went bankrupt or lost most of their fortunes because of national and economic complications later. But that was all in the future when the pitcher bearing the Norfolk merchant's recognition flags was new. And, in the meantime, prosperity reigned in the countinghouses and warehouses along Norfolk's waterfront.

As a result of the French Revolution, war broke out all over Europe, and as the merchant fleet of Great Britain was too busy conveying military supplies to ports other than the West Indies, the people of those islands were faced with starvation unless vital foodstuffs were imported from the United States.

Since Virginia had those supplies in abundance, the governing bodies of the islands disregarded the Navigation Acts, which forbade the importation of commodities into the British dependencies in other than British bottoms, and welcomed the ships of the Norfolk merchants.

In exchange for grain, flour, beef, pork, lumber, and other supplies, the Norfolk vessels brought back all manner of exotic cargoes, ranging from great logs of Santo Domingo mahogany to puncheons of St. Kitt's rum.

But Norfolk's commercial supremacy of that period was short-lived. President Jefferson's embargo on foreign trade as a retaliatory measure against Great Britain; the War of 1812; the capture of Norfolk vessels by French privateers (the French Spoliation); and the opening of the Erie Canal, which easily gave New York precedence over all of the Atlantic ports—each contributed to the ruin of Norfolk's once prosperous merchants.

The following observation, taken from the Norfolk Gazette and Public Ledger of January 4, 1815 is sufficient comment on what happened.

"Some years ago walking through Wide Water Street, I was much incommoded by rum puncheons, sugar hogsheads, bales of goods, flour and tobacco hogsheads. I heard the bawling of Negroes as they hoisted these goods in and out of vessels, and I got the odor of tar and turpentine. I was in constant danger of breaking my shins on the skids of passing drays. Recently I again went through Water Street, Market Square, and Main Street. No rum puncheons, no bales of goods, no sugar and tobacco hogsheads, no bawling Negroes, no drays passing. Instead of plodding merchants, and busy clerks, I saw only some military officers, ten or twelve idle youths, a few recruits, and a group of Negroes. From the nearby dram shops came the fumes of egg-nog and cigars, and the sound of fiddles and tamborines."

Chapter Twenty-nine

Decatur Drinks a Famous Toast

Time-honored tradition, sanctioned by all of the standard books of quotations on the market, says that when Commodore Stephen Decatur lifted his glass at a testimonial dinner given in his honor in Norfolk on April 4, 1816, he said: "Our Country! In her intercourse with foreign nations, may she always be in the right, but our country right or wrong."

But that is not what Decatur said, according to the two contemporary Norfolk newspaper accounts of the affair that have been preserved. The first of these is in the American Beacon (a daily) in its issue of the day after the banquet. The second is in the Norfolk Gazette & Public Ledger (a triweekly) that appeared two days after the affair.

Both reported that when Decatur's time came to propose a toast, he lifted his glass and said: "Our country! In her intercourse with foreign nations, may she always be in the right, and always successful, right or wrong."

Decatur was at the zenith of his distinguished naval career when he proposed the toast. The American naval hero of the hour, he had just returned to the United States as the commanding officer of a squadron that had successfully settled the Mediterranean maritime troubles that had plagued American commerce for two decades. Everywhere the thirty-seven-year-old hero went he was lionized, and he remained the naval darling of the nation until his tragic death in the famous duel in 1820 with Commodore James Barron.

On April 4, 1816, the day Decatur was wined and dined in Norfolk, he was treated as the hero of the hour.

Under the head of "Tribute to Valour and Patriotism," the American Beacon of April 5, 1816, said: "Yesterday our citizens testified to Commodore Stephen Decatur, by a Public Dinner, the exalted sense they entertain of his galantry and public services."

The "neat and plentiful dinner," well supplied with wines and liquors, was provided by Matthew Glenn of the Exchange Hotel on Main Street and was served in the assembly room of the establishment.

A company of one hundred and twenty "officers of the Navy and Army of this station" and the "most representative citizens of this borough" sat down to the table at 5 p.m. John Nivison, a well known Norfolk attorney, presided. He was assisted by his son-in-law, Littleton Waller Tazewell, also a prominent member of the Norfolk bar.

According to the Beacon, "the utmost cordiality and harmony prevailed," and after the meal was over, eighteen prepared toasts were drunk. After the glasses had clinked over the last one, Decatur was invited to propose an extemporaneous toast. It was then that he responded with the salute to his country that has been misquoted for so many years.

As a final gesture, the guests sang a two-verse song written for the occasion by a citizen of Petersburg. The tune used was "To Anacreon in Heaven," the same melody Francis Scott Key used for the musical setting of "The Star Spangled Banner."

The second verse paid particular tribute to Decatur:

"Algiers' haughty Dey, in the height of his pride,
From American freemen a tribute demanded;
Columbia's brave freemen the tribute denied,

And his Corsairs to seize our bold tars was commanded.
Their streamers wave high,
For Decatur draws nigh,
His name strikes like lightning—in terror they fly—
Thrice welcome our hero, returned from afar.
Where the proud crescent falls to the American Star."

Chapter Thirty

The Chesapeake-Leopard Affair

The prelude and epilogue of the Chesapeake-Leopard affair
that came close to causing hostilities between the United States
and Great Britain took place in Norfolk.

On June 22, 1807, the United States frigate Chesapeake
cleared Norfolk area waters for the Mediterranean to relieve the
USS Constitution as flagship of the European station. In
command was Captain (later Commodore) James Barron, who
had been the senior officer aboard for only one day.

The Chesapeake was badly prepared for her mission. Her
crew was shorthanded and untrained, her decks were littered
with unstowed gear, and her powder flasks and loggerheads were
stored away in her hold.

Standing down Thimble Shoals Channel, the Chesapeake
passed a British squadron anchored in Lynnhaven Roads.
Catching sight of the Chesapeake, one of the British vessels, the
HMS Leopard, weighed anchor and followed her.

Side by side the two ships sailed to about forty miles at sea,
at which point the Leopard passed the Chesapeake, then backed
a topsail and waited until the Chesapeake came down to her.
At that point a British lieutenant was rowed over to the
Chesapeake in a small boat. When he came aboard and was
taken to Captain Barron, he informed the latter that his ship
would have to submit to a search for supposed deserters from
the Royal Navy who were believed to be on board. Barron

naturally refused to comply, and the British lieutenant was rowed back to the Leopard.

Seeing that the Leopard's gunports were open and her guns were run out, Barron and his officers made a frantic effort to prepare the Chesapeake for resistance, but they were hindered by the unprepared condition of the vessel's armament. The Leopard then blazed away at the Chesapeake for fifteen minutes, killing three men and wounding eighteen before Barron struck his colors. The British lieutenant then returned to Barron's riddled ship and took out three men whom the British claimed were deserters, plus a fourth man for good measure.

When the news of the incident filtered back into Norfolk, enraged citizens swarmed out in rowboats to every vessel which came in from the Virginia Capes to question their crews and passengers. Finally, when they saw a vessel approaching carrying eleven wounded men from the Chesapeake, all doubts were dispelled.

Seeking immediate revenge, Norfolk citizens held a mass meeting at which it was unanimously agreed to refuse all intercourse with any of the British men of war in the area, either by providing them with pilots or by selling them supplies or water. In the meantime, a subscription was gotten up for the families of the men who had been killed by the Leopard's guns.

On June 27, 1807, when Robert MacDonald, one of the wounded Chesapeake sailors, died in the Marine Hospital at Washington Point, later known as Berkley, his funeral in Norfolk became the occasion of a great public demonstration.

As his body was ferried across the river to the County Wharf, all of the American vessels in the harbor displayed their colors at half mast, while minute guns were fired by the artillery on shore. An estimated four thousand citizens were waiting on Market Square, and while the coffin was being landed, they formed themselves into a long procession.

The cortege was made up of the coffin accompanied by masters of vessels in the harbor who had been selected as pall-bearers, borough officials and military companies, and captains, mates, and seamen from other vessels. These and the long line of citizens then marched to the measure of muffled drums to the first Christ Church on Church Street for an elaborate funeral service in MacDonald's honor.

Chapter Thirty-one

Historic Fort Norfolk

Fort Norfolk, a bastion that never blazed away at an enemy, houses one of the oldest government agencies in the Norfolk area.

Established during the Revolution, the fort was the headquarters for the defense of Norfolk in the War of 1812, saw the Virginia (Merrimack) steam down to Hampton Roads in 1862 for her historic encounter with the Monitor, served as a Civil War prison, and finally became the headquarters of the Norfolk District of the Army Corps of Engineers in 1923.

In point of age, Fort Norfolk is only a few months younger than the agency it houses within its thick, old, whitewashed walls. The Corps of Engineers was established on June 16, 1775, a few months before the fort was begun.

Located at that point on the Elizabeth River known as "The Narrows," where the river fans out to the eastward to form Norfolk's inner harbor, Fort Norfolk is opposite the Portsmouth Naval Hospital, the site of Fort Nelson, another Revolutionary fort. Although Fort Nelson was still in good condition in 1824, when an Army survey of both forts was made, all traces of it have disappeared. Fort Norfolk, however, except for the addition of a few modern buildings, is practically the same as it was then.

Fort Norfolk was established by the State of Virginia shortly after the burning of Norfolk in January of 1776. The Virginia forces, however, made the mistake of manning it too lightly. And when Sir George Collier sailed up the Elizabeth River in May of 1779 with a large British fleet, the garrison was unable to offer any resistance.

On March 4, 1794, President George Washington was authorized to build a series of forts to protect nineteen United States harbors. One year later, on May 21, 1795, Edward and Sarah Poole sold the property on which the Revolutionary fort had stood to the United States government for two hundred pounds sterling, after which Fort Norfolk as it appears today was begun.

In 1807, when the second war with Great Britain was brewing, the people of Norfolk began to fortify the city and put Fort Norfolk in repair. Large quantities of gunpowder and stores were collected there, and a heavy chain was stretched across the river from the fort to Fort Nelson to prevent British warships from entering Norfolk's inner harbor.

War did not come to the Norfolk area, however, until February of 1813, when Admiral Sir George Cockburn brought a British squadron into the Virginia Capes to blockade the Chesapeake Bay. Before it fled the U. S. frigate Constellation, crowding on every available inch of canvas to reach the protection of the guns of Fort Norfolk. In her haste, she missed the channel and ran aground, but hundreds of Norfolk citizens came down the river in small boats and lightened her until she floated to safety.

The Constellation remained at Norfolk throughout the war, aiding greatly in its defense with her officers, crew, guns, and small boats.

General Robert Barraud Taylor, later the first judge of the Superior Court of Law and Chancery for the Borough of Norfolk, the forerunner of the present Norfolk Court of Law and Chancery, was Fort Norfolk's commander during the exciting times of 1812-1814.

Following the war of 1812, Fort Norfolk's history was humdrum until the Civil War. when a Confederate battery was erected there. After the fall of Norfolk to the Federal forces in May of 1862, it was used by them as a prison until March of 1863, when General Benjamin F. Butler transferred it to the Navy. The Navy retained the fort for many decades, although the Army Corps of Engineers made use of it at various times. Since it was formally turned over to the Corps of Engineers in 1923, the damage caused by years of neglect has been repaired, and the site now constitutes a quiet, green oasis on the northern side of the Elizabeth River's hustle and bustle of heavy traffic.

Chapter Thirty-two

The Battle of Craney Island

Craney Island at the mouth of the Elizabeth River, the scene of the American victory that spared Norfolk from being captured by the British during the War of 1812, was originally known as Crayne or Craney Point.

The name was derived from the fact that the early settlers on the Elizabeth River were impressed with the great number of what they mistakenly believed to be cranes that inhabited it. Hence the name Crayne or Craney Point, although the birds the settlers thought were cranes were actually white and blue herons, still fairly common birds in the Tidewater area.

After an uneventful Colonial history, Craney Island came into its own in 1813 when an American force stationed there successfully repelled a British attack during this country's second war with England. In February of 1813 an impressive British squadron commanded by Admiral Sir George Cockburn sailed through the Virginia Capes to blockade the Chesapeake Bay.

This action bottled up the U. S. frigate Constellation in Norfolk harbor. But this was a blessing in disguise as the officers, sailors, marines, guns, and small boats of the frigate proved invaluable in defending Norfolk from the blockaders.

The appearance of the British in Norfolk-area waters hurried the preparations for defense, the coordination of which was placed under the command of General Robert Barraud Taylor of Norfolk. Fortifications on the outskirts of Norfolk and Portsmouth were hastily thrown up, but Taylor had no idea of letting the enemy get that close to home if he could help it.

Commandeering every vessel he could, Taylor threw a floating barrier across the mouth of the Elizabeth River, while Craney Island was strengthened with a fort and redoubts. These were manned by personnel from the Constellation and two companies of light artillery, one of which was commanded by Captain Arthur Emmerson of Portsmouth.

On June 21, 1813, the already formidable British fleet was strengthened by new arrivals, after which the entire squadron moved up to the mouth of the Nansemond River.

Early on the morning of June 22, 1813, a long drum roll in the American ranks announced that the British had launched a ground attack on the western side of the island. In the excitement, the defenders realized that they were not displaying a flag, so a pole was hastily hunted up, an American flag was nailed to its top, and it was hoisted over the breastworks.

About two thousand British took part in the land attack, but the American fire was so deadly that they eventually fell back with heavy losses. In the meantime, an attack was launched on the river side of the island by a double column of fifty British barges, led by the fifty-two-foot barge, Centipede, a handsome craft with a shining brass three-pounder in its bow.

Waiting until the floating attack was well within range of his guns, Captain Emmerson finally yelled, "Now my brave boys, are you ready? Fire!"

The result was lethal, and the barges were sunk and scattered like so many sitting ducks. In all, the British lost around two hundred men and the defenders not one.

The American victory at Craney Island saved Norfolk and Portsmouth from being captured and pillaged by the enemy. Commenting on the bravery of the defenders, General Taylor wrote the United States Secretary of War:

"The courage and constancy with which this inferior force, in the face of a formidable naval armament, not only sustained a position in which nothing was complete, but repelled the enemy with considerable loss, cannot fail to command the approbation of the government and the applause of their country."

Chapter Thirty-three

Lafayette's Four Visits

Lafayette visited Norfolk four times during his last triumphant visit to the United States in 1824-25. On the first occasion he was the official guest of the borough. The other times he was just passing through on his way to other places.

Lafayette left Alexandria aboard the steamboat Petersburg on his way to Norfolk for his official visit on October 17, 1824. On the way he stopped over at Yorktown for a two-day gala celebration of the forty-third anniversary of the surrender of Cornwallis, at which General Robert Barraud Taylor of Norfolk was one of the principal speakers. Proceeding to Jamestown by way of Williamsburg, Lafayette was met on the morning of Friday, October 22, 1824, by a delegation from Norfolk. And after "a sumptuous collation was served" aboard the Petersburg, the party left for Norfolk.

It was a never-to-be-forgotten day in the borough, and thousands had come from miles around to welcome the hero of the Revolution. At 5 p.m., a lookout who had been posted for the purpose sighted the Petersburg. And as soon as the signal was given, Norfolk's inner harbor resounded with salvos of artillery.

Anchoring in midstream, the Petersburg was met by an

elegantly decorated 18-oared barge in which the Nation's Guest and his suite were rowed to the foot of Market Square that was brave with the colorful uniforms of the local military and the bright Sunday-go-to-meeting clothes of the people who crowded every available foot of space, peered from every window, and perched precariously on rooftops to get a glimpse of the old hero.

Lafayette was welcomed to the borough, under a specially constructed arch at the head of Market Square, by Norfolk Mayor John E. Holt, after which he was driven to Mrs. Hansford's boarding house at Main and East streets where suitably elegant quarters had been prepared for him. That evening the borough was ablaze with candles, lamps, and transparencies, while forty-two bonfires turned night into day along the waterfront.

On Saturday morning, Lafayette held a "levee," after which he and three hundred invited guests dined at the Exchange Hotel to the music of the Mozart Amateur Band. Then, when the last toast was drunk, Lafayette accompanied General Taylor to his home, "where he supped in company with a numerous party." On Sunday morning, Lafayette attended services at Christ Church on Church Street, and that afternoon he left for a visit to Fort Monroe.

In describing this visit, Captain Rufus Baker of the Engineers wrote to his mother, "Gen. Lafayette visited our post, stayed all night with us—reviewed our Regiment, and eat and drank — and then eat and drank again — In fact, Mother — he eats like an Alderman, and always has a keen appetite for duplicate dinners, suppers & breakfasts — and I am told that he considers York river oysters that fill a tumbler—as mere vegetables."

On Monday, October 25, 1824, Lafayette visited Castle Calhoun (the Rip Raps), Portsmouth, and the Gosport Navy Yard. That night he was entertained by his Norfolk hosts at a grand ball in the new Customs House at Church and Water streets which he left at 11:30 p.m. to take a steamboat for Richmond, "quitting the ballroom, where everything partook of joy and gratitude."

Lafayette passed through Norfolk on three other occasions. On January 21, 1825, he was again in Norfolk for a few hours on his way from Baltimore to Richmond to attend a session of the Virginia Legislature. Six days later, he arrived in Norfolk again from Richmond on his way back to Baltimore, at which time he was entertained at breakfast by the borough authorities at Carr's Hotel on Main Street.

Lafayette passed through Norfolk for the last time on February 25, 1825, when he arrived from Washington aboard the steamboat Potomac and left around noon the same day in Thompson's Stage for Suffolk on the first leg of his Southern tour.

Chapter Thirty-four

The Norfolk-Portsmouth Ferries

The Gosport, a "neat and handsome vessel," built in Portsmouth and outfitted with her engine in Philadelphia, was the first steam ferry to run between Norfolk and Portsmouth. She made her first trips across the harbor in 1832, taking five minutes, then considered a fast trip, to navigate from wharf to wharf.

At that time, however, Norfolk already had a ferry history dating from 1636, when Captain Adam Thorowgood had set up the first convenience of its sort south of Hampton Roads, using a crude, hand-rowed skiff to replace the hit-or-miss log canoe navigation of the Indians.

The appearance of the Gosport in Norfolk harbor established a tradition of regular service that was terminated one hundred and twenty-three years later on August 31, 1955, when the last Norfolk-Portsmouth ferry ran.

Before the coming of steam, the Norfolk-Portsmouth ferries

were first serviced by man-powered boats, and later with larger craft equipped with paddle wheels driven by blind mules or horses on a treadmill. During the latter period, according to tradition, the man who leased the ferries made a point to hire only one-legged men to row the boats. On one occasion when a persistent two-legged man kept insisting on being given a job, the ferry captain got rid of him by grabbing a saw and making a dive for the applicant's right leg. At that point, the insistent seeker of employment sought a job elsewhere.

Once the puffing old tubs took over the harbor, many colorful events took place that contributed greatly to the folklore of the Norfolk area.

Shortly after steam replaced manpower, mulepower, and horsepower on the ferry run, an unsuspecting Norfolk area citizen, according to tradition, wound up wishing that he hadn't been so curious. Mistaking a brass-bound exhaust pipe projecting from the wall of one of the Gosport's successors as a speaking tube, he carried on a one-way conversation until a gush of steam from the boiler room resulted in his being presented with a set of false teeth by the ferry officials.

Then there was the Manahassett, a popular side-wheeler that was known as the "Mammy Ferry." The upper deck of this boat was enclosed in lattice work, making it a safe place for children to play while riding across the harbor.

Every sunny summer afternoon while the Manahassett was plying the harbor, her upper deck was reserved for Norfolk area nursemaids. And after the gate leading to the upper deck had been locked by a deckhand, they would settle down for a leisurely gossip in the checquered sunlight while their charges romped all over the upper deck for an inclusive fare of twenty-five cents per party for the entire afternoon.

There was also the Confederate flag incident which took place when the Federal forces were operating the ferries from 1862 to 1865. Hoping to humiliate the Confederate sympathizers in Norfolk and Portsmouth, some of the soldiers guarding the

Portsmouth ferry terminal stretched the Stars and Bars across the floor at the entrance of the ticket booth.

During the ensuing melee, a loyal Southern girl snatched up the flag, secreted it in her muff, and escaped before she could be apprehended.

One of the best stories concerning the old ferries, however, dates from the early 1850s, when a male passenger strenuously objected in the press to the obscene drawings and graffiti he found on the waiting room walls during his crossings of the harbor. Taking the hint, the ferry management promised to have the room whitewashed every week. But it also added a footnote for the benefit of the prudish bellyacher:

"Go into the waiting room and sit quietly down," it admonished, "not wasting your time reading the scribbling on the wall."

Chapter Thirty-five

The Making of a Shrine

When the former Norfolk Court House and City Hall was renovated as a memorial to General of the Army Douglas MacArthur and opened to the public in January of 1964, an earlier Norfolk tourist custom was reversed.

Four years after the completion of the building in 1850, visitors climbed the two flights of steps leading to its cupola, the highest point of vantage in the city, to get a bird's-eye view of the town and its harbor. Now tourists concentrate on the tomb of the general and the souvenirs of his military career displayed below in the area that once resounded with the gavels of justice.

The Classic Revival Court House was the architectural symbol of Norfolk's new dignity, acquired on February 13, 1845, when the Virginia General Assembly passed an act changing its status from a borough to that of a city.

The handsome building that housed Norfolk's courts for more than a century and was the scene of many stirring trials and other historic events was first occupied by "the Worshipful Court of the City of Norfolk" on May 20, 1850. Judge Richard Baker was the first to occupy the bench there.

In commenting on the opening of the building, the Daily Southern Argus took the judge to task for his dilatory manner of dispensing justice. "With all deference and respect," it said, "we hope Judge Baker will turn over a new leaf to insure a more prompt and efficient administration of the laws. As business is now conducted, it not only involves much delay and expense, but in many cases amounts to absolute denial of justice."

The Court House cost $50,000 to build and was erected on made ground, the site being part of what was formerly known as Town Back Creek.

On February 27, 1833, the Virginia General Assembly authorized the Borough of Norfolk to fill in that portion of the waterway extending east from the present Bank Street. At that time the Norfolk Borough Court House stood on East Main Street on the site later occupied by the Norfolk Union Mission. This court house was erected during 1790-91 and remained in use until the Court House facing on Bank Street was occupied.

By 1837, the site of the Court House, now the MacArthur Memorial, had been reclaimed from the waters of Town Back Creek, and by 1845 the city fathers were thinking in terms of the new building. On April 23, 1846, the issue was put to a vote, and Norfolk citizens approved the reclaimed land as a site for the building. Five months later, the Norfolk Common Council voted to go ahead with the building and paid William R. Singleton one hundred dollars for the plans he had prepared for it.

Singleton was one of the foremost American architects of his time. A native of Portsmouth, he was practicing in St. Louis, Missouri, at that time. His plans for the Norfolk County Court House in Portsmouth had made such a favorable impression that the Norfolk Council chose him.

Money for the new building was raised by selling the old Borough Court House on Main Street and by assessing each qualified Norfolk voter one dollar. Piles for the building were driven between May and July of 1847, and by the end of August the work had progressed sufficiently on the foundations for the cornerstone to be laid.

The parade that preceded the ceremony was pronounced by the newspapers to be the largest public procession in the history of the city. Lodge members in full regalia, military companies, naval officers, Norfolk area clergymen, and other prominent citizens rode in carriages or walked in the parade to the music of several bands.

The Masons conducted the cornerstone-laying ceremony, and the Reverend A. L. Hitzelberger, the pastor of Norfolk's St. Patrick's Catholic Church, "delivered an address which was characterized by elegance of style, combined with highly appropriate and classical allusions, and patriotic sentiments."

Chapter Thirty-six

The 1855 Yellow Fever Epidemic

The 1855 yellow fever epidemic, referred to by contemporaries as "The Death Storm," that wiped out around two thousand of Norfolk's population, was one of the worst disasters in the history of the city.

Norfolk had previously experienced bad outbreaks of "Yellow Jack"—notably in 1795, 1802, 1821, and 1826—but none of them could compare with the epidemic of 1855. Then, on June 7, 1855, the steamer Ben Franklin, en route to New York from St. Thomas in the Virgin Islands, where a yellow fever epidemic was raging, put into Hampton Roads in distress. Her hold, containing the larvae of the deadly yellow fever transmitting mosquito, the Ades aegypti, was a veritable Pandora's Box of pestilential evil.

The Ben Franklin was quarantined in Hampton Roads until June 19, when the health authorities permitted her captain to take her to Page and Allen's shipyard near the Gosport Navy Yard on the condition that her hold "was not to be broken up." After tying up at the shipyard, however, the captain violated his promise and had the hatches opened and the bilges pumped out.

The first man stricken was a Richmond machinist named Carter who was working in the ship's hold. On July 5, he came down with the fever, and three days later he died. His death was followed by an outbreak of the fever in a crowded nearby tenement known as "Irish Row," from which it spread into Portsmouth.

When "Irish Row" was closed by the health authorities, Norfolk gave shelter to some of the families that had been evicted from the slum and quartered them in an equally rundown tenement on South Church Street known as "Barry's Row." It was there that the fever broke out in Norfolk on July 30, after which it spread rapidly throughout the city.

At that point, a general exodus to escape from the dread disease began. But before long many cities, notably New York, Richmond, and Petersburg, which had at first welcomed the refugees, refused to receive any others from the pestilence-stricken Norfolk area. It is also a matter of record that a boatload of refugees was repulsed at bayonet-point while attempting to land at Old Point.

There were other communities, however, notably the Virginia Eastern Shore, Mathews County, and Fredericksburg, that gave asylum to those fleeing from the fever. And soon, moved by accounts of the pitiful plight of Norfolk that appeared in the nation's press, volunteers from all over the country came to Norfolk to nurse the stricken, while substantial sums of money were collected to assist the fever-racked community.

August 14 was set aside by the authorities as a day of humiliation and prayer, but the fever continued to rage. And before the end of August all business in Norfolk had been suspended and the city was one great hospital. The only vessel entering the Norfolk harbor at that time was the little steamer J. E. Coffee that met boats from Baltimore and Richmond in Hampton Roads to pick up the mail and bring in coffins. Before long, however, coffins became a luxury, and the bodies of the fever victims had to be buried in boxes or in the blankets in which they had died.

Many Norfolkians, because of their untiring efforts, became legendary heroes during the epidemic, notably the Reverend Matthew O'Keefe, pastor of St. Patrick's Catholic Church, and Dr. George D. Armstrong, the Norfolk Presbyterian minister. Armstrong later wrote a fascinating account of his experiences, "A History of the Ravages of the Yellow Fever in Norfolk, Virginia, A.D. 1855," that describes the ninety-day terror in graphic detail. And although he had no idea that the wind-borne mosquito was the agent of transmission of the fever, he came close to pinpointing the cause when he observed: "The disease . . . spread rapidly in the direction of the prevailing winds and but slowly in a direction across the track of those winds."

Finally, with the coming of frost, the epidemic ended. Of those who survived, according to Burton's "History of Norfolk," "every man, woman and child, almost without exception had been stricken by the fell fever, and about 2,000 had been buried."

Chapter Thirty-seven

Two Memorable Freezes

Two memorable freezes gripped Norfolk in their icy clutches during the Eighteenth and Nineteenth Centuries. The first was the rigorous winter of 1779-80, during which the Elizabeth River was frozen solid for several weeks and the Chesapeake Bay was so thickly frozen that teams crossed from shore to shore as far down as Cape Henry.

It was also during this freeze that the coldest morning ever known in Virginia since the time of the first settlement was experienced. On January 14, 1780, the mercury dropped into the bulbs of the thermometers, while ice piled up twenty feet high along the Atlantic Coast in Princess Anne County and remained there until mid-May.

Seventy-seven years later Norfolk area citizens who liked to bend the elbow were treating themselves to the unique experience of taking a hot toddy at a temporary bar set up in the middle of the Elizabeth River.

It all began on Friday, January 16, 1857. Although there had been several inches of snow and the usual bad weather on New Year's Day, the editor of The Southern Argus, on the strength of "two delicious mint julips from the Anchor Bar," had forgotten it sufficiently to hail the first signs of spring. By the next morning, however, the wind had veered around to the northeast, and at half past eleven snow began to fall rapidly. By noon the temperature had dropped to an all-time low and a furious gale sent snowflakes whirling in all directions. The great blizzard and freeze of 1857 were on!

Two days later, Norfolk and Portsmouth were buried under twenty-foot snowdrifts, and the damage of the storm to the two cities was roughly estimated at one hundred thousand dollars. Added to that, the Elizabeth River was a blinding surface of hard, gray ice, while the cold had become so intense that all of the Virginia rivers and Hampton Roads were ice-bound.

Chesapeake Bay was frozen solid for a mile and a half from the shoreline, and at Cape Henry it was possible to walk out a hundred yards on the frozen ocean from the lighthouse.

The suffering among the Norfolk-area poor was terrible, but in middle-income and well-to-do Norfolk families an ice carnival spirit prevailed.

Sleighing and skating parties were organized throughout the community, and a pair of skates, a sled, or a sleigh of any description sold at a premium.

On January 26, 1857, the Argus announced that many persons had walked all the way down to Hampton Roads on the ice over the weekend, while one hardy soul had strolled twenty miles from Nansemond County on the ice, had dined with the captain of an ice-bound steamer off Craney Island, and had then finished his promenade to Norfolk.

"Our harbor has been converted into a magnificent panorama," the Argus commented. "On Saturday, belles and beaux, husbands and wives, parents and children all crowded the thoroughfare on the ice between Norfolk and Portsmouth."

Then came the real news of the day: "A booth was erected about midway of the journey where thirsty souls imbibed the ardent, and a brisk trade was carried on beneath it."

This was the famous "bar in the center of the river," part of the folklore of every Nineteenth Century Norfolk-area person.

Needless to add, "the ardent," as the editor of the Argus referred to the liquid refreshment served over the bar on the ice, was the cause of many fights and cases of unsteady legs. And according to tradition, although the editor of the Argus had nothing to say concerning it, a free Negro family in Portsmouth pressed their small donkey cart into service and piled up a tidy little sum transporting the drunks backward and forward to terra firma.

By January 28, 1857, however, the thaw had begun, and the next day the ferryboat made several cautious crossings through a path cut through the melting ice. With things back to normal, the ice carnival spirit quieted down, and was not revived until the big freeze of 1917-18, when the harbor again became a solid mass of ice between Norfolk and Portsmouth.

Chapter Thirty-eight

Landmark of Loveliness

St. Mary of the Immaculate Conception, Norfolk's oldest and most beautiful Catholic church, was one of the first churches in the United States to be named for the dogma of the Immaculate Conception. The belief that the Virgin Mary was free of original sin from the time of her conception was an ancient Catholic one, but it was not until December 8, 1854, that Pope Pius IX defined it as a dogma.

Two years later, on December 6, 1856, St. Patrick's, Norfolk's second Catholic church, was destroyed by fire. And when it was replaced by the present church at Holt and Chapel streets, the new church was consecrated on October 3, 1858, by the Right Reverend John McGill, bishop of the Diocese of Richmond, as St. Mary of the Immaculate Conception.

The history of Catholicism in Norfolk dates from August 1791, when the Reverend Jean Dubois, accompanied by several priests and other refugees, arrived in Norfolk from revolution-torn France. Three years later the "Roman Catholic Society of Norfolk Borough" bought the property on which St. Mary's now stands.

On this site a small chapel, Norfolk's first Catholic church, was built and a cemetery was established. This building gave the name Chapel Street to the then newly created thoroughfare that it faced. The simple chapel was replaced in 1842 by St. Patrick's, a handsome Greek Revival building with an imposing classic portico that stood on Holt Street just behind the present St. Mary's until it burned in 1856.

At the time of the fire, the Reverend Matthew O'Keefe was in charge of the Norfolk Catholic congregation. Father O'Keefe had endeared himself to the people of Norfolk for his heroic service during the 1855 yellow fever epidemic. And when he appealed for funds to rebuild his church, Catholics and Protestants worked untiringly to raise the money.

The total cost of the undertaking was sixty-five thousand dollars, and the congregation was left badly in debt. As a result, from 1858 to 1874, Father O'Keefe drew no salary while this debt was being reduced. The combined efforts of Father O'Keefe and his Norfolk friends and parishioners were so successful, however, that the new church, the tall cross-crowned steeple of which is one of the few remaining old landmarks on the downtown Norfolk skyline, was ready for dedication in less than two years.

Despite careful research, the name of the architect of St. Mary's has never been discovered, but whoever was responsible for its soaring architectural distinction did his work well. For none other than Ralph Adams Cram, the famous American architect and medievalist, who visited it in the early 1900s, called it "the best ante-bellum Gothic workmanship in the South."

Elegantly proportioned on the outside, St. Mary's has an interior that is breathtakingly beautiful. Delicate clustered columns crowned by elaborately fashioned capitals support its pointed arched Gothic roof, studded at intervals with symbolic bosses in gilded plaster.

Also notable are its fourteen Stations of the Cross painted in oil on copper by L. Chevot of Paris, the handsome choir loft at the back of the church containing its original tracker-type organ, the black and white marble paving of its aisles, and its handsome brass and marble baptismal font. The three altars of the church are also lovely, particularly the main altar, a marvelous Victorian sculptural fantasy of Carrara marble and Brazilian onyx.

But the main glory of St. Mary's is its magnificent stained-glass windows, regarded by many as the finest in Virginia.

Created specially for the church by Mayer Studios of Munich, Germany, the windows were installed in 1918. And even on the darkest days they transform the interior of St. Mary's into a sanctuary of bejewelled wonder.

Chapter Thirty-nine

Alexander Galt—The Sculptor from Norfolk

Alexander Galt, one of the best-known American sculptors of his day, was Norfolk's first bid for national artistic fame.

Born in Norfolk on January 26, 1827, Galt was a son of Alexander Galt Sr., Norfolk's postmaster at that time. His artistic talents were first noticed when he was a pupil of a Frenchman, M. Schisano, whose school was a well-known Norfolk institution of its day.

Galt's first efforts at sculpture were miniature figures carved from pieces of chalk he carried in his pockets to chalk the taws he used when shooting marbles with his schoolmates. From these he progressed to small alabaster figures, after which he began carving cameos from conch shells, several of which were set in gold and worn by Norfolk belles of that era.

Galt's talents continued to develop rapidly, and when he was twenty-one he realized his boyhood ambition of going to Florence, Italy, to study sculpture.

By 1853, when he was twenty-six, Galt was an established sculptor, and the two works he exhibited at the Crystal Palace exhibition in New York of that year attracted considerable attention. One of these, an allegorical marble bust called "Virginia," was purchased for two hundred and fifty dollars by the Art Union of New York.

Galt's principal work, and the one by which he is best remembered today, was a life-size marble statue of Thomas Jefferson commissioned by the Virginia General Assembly in 1854 as a gift to the University of Virginia. Upon completion, the statue, for which Galt received ten thousand dollars, was brought back to Richmond, where it was exhibited against a scarlet cloth background illuminated with gaslights.

After the Civil War, it was placed in the Rotunda of the University where it remained until 1895, when the building was damaged by fire. After the restoration of the building, it was returned to its former place of honor.

An ardent Southerner, Galt sided with his native Virginia at the outbreak of the Civil War. In 1862, when he was visiting Stonewall Jackson's camp to take measurements of the general for a proposed statue, he contracted smallpox. He died early in 1863 in Richmond and was buried in Hollywood Cemetery there.

Fortunately, his correspondence, sketchbooks, diaries, and other papers were carefully preserved by his family and are now in the library of the University of Virginia.

Romantically classical by temperament, Galt drew his inspiration from ancient Greece and Rome. One of his works, an ideal bust of Sappho, has an interesting story.

Commissioned by the Norfolk-born Virginia historian, Hugh Blair Grigsby, the bust was shipped from Italy to New York early in 1861.

The Civil War had begun when it arrived, and as it was Southern property, it was confiscated and sold to J. Nelson Tappan, a wealthy New York merchant.

After the war, Grigsby went to New York in search of the bust, and when he discovered it and presented Tappan with the evidence that he was the rightful owner, the New Yorker graciously turned it over to him, refusing any remuneration.

The bust was then shipped to Norfolk, where Grigsby installed it in the drawing room of his halfbrother, the banker, John B. Whitehead, where it was acclaimed the finest art work in the city until Grigsby sent it to his country home in Charlotte County.

Chapter Forty

Other Notable Buildings and Houses

Besides the MacArthur Memorial and several old downtown churches that are still used by their original congregations, Norfolk has three other outstanding old public buildings and six architecturally distinctive early houses.

The oldest public building is Old Christ Church at Cumberland and Freemason streets. Once the most fashionable house of worship in Norfolk, it is now sadly run down. It was consecrated on November 9, 1828, and replaced the first Christ Church on Church Street, built in 1800 and burned in 1827. Its architect was Thomas Williamson (1776-1846), the cashier of the Virginia Bank in Norfolk and an amateur architect.

Next in point of age is the Old Norfolk Academy on Bank Street. It was modeled by its architect, Thomas Ustic Walter (1804-1887) of Philadelphia, on the Theseum in Athens. Its cornerstone was laid on May 25, 1840, and it was opened in 1841. During the 1855 yellow fever epidemic it was used temporarily as Norfolk's Post Office.

The Norfolk Customs House is the city's third outstanding old public building. Designed by Ami B. Young (1798-1874), a government architect, the dignified Blue Hill granite building with an elevated pedimented Roman Corinthian portico was begun in 1852 and completed in 1859.

The Taylor-Whittle House at Freemason and Duke streets, the first of the six architecturally distinctive old houses, not only is one of Norfolk's oldest houses but also is considered one of the finest examples of Federal architecture in the country. It stands on confiscated Tory property that was later granted in 1788 to George Purdie, who had also been accused unjustly during the Revolution of having Tory sympathies. Tradition says the man who built the house, presumably Purdie, never lived in it. In any event, it was occupied by John Cowper, a Norfolk merchant and mayor of Norfolk in 1801, when he deeded it on December 15, 1802, to Richard Taylor (1771-1827), the ancestor of its later occupants.

The Boush-Tazewell House, dating from the 1780s, that formerly stood on the site of the Colonial Theater in downtown Norfolk but was moved during the early Twentieth Century to Edgewater, is also one of Norfolk's historic homes. Its most notable occupant was Littleton Waller Tazewell (1774-1860), a former United States senator and governor of Virginia.

The Myers House at Freemason and Bank streets, built in 1792 on property acquired in September 1791 by Moses Myers, one of Norfolk's early merchant princes, is also an outstanding example of Federal architecture. The addition containing the octagonal end dining room, considered one of the finest rooms of its period in the country, was added about ten years after the original house was built. Many notables, including Lafayette, James Monroe, Stephen Decatur, and President Theodore Roosevelt, have been entertained there.

The nearby Willoughby-Baylor House, dating from the closing years of the Eighteenth Century, was built on the site of Norfolk's pre-Revolutionary "Mason's Hall." It was originally owned by Captain William Willoughby and later was occupied by several generations of the Baylor family.

The Allmand-Archer House on Duke Street was built in the 1790s by Matthew Heary, who sold it in 1802 to Harrison Allmand, a Norfolk merchant who was known as "Old Gold Dust" because of his great wealth. It was used as headquarters for American officers during the War of 1812 and is still owned by Allmand's descendants.

The Selden House at Freemason and Botetourt streets was built in 1807 by Dr. William Boswell Selden as a country house when that part of Freemason Street was known as Grafton Street. Selden's son, Dr. William Selden, entertained General Robert E. Lee there in 1870.

The Lamb House on West Bute Street, originally known as

"Kenmure" from a family estate in Scotland, dates from 1845. Its builder, William Wilson Lamb, was mayor of Norfolk in 1862 when the city was recaptured by the Federal forces. Norfolk's historic Mace was hidden by Lamb under one of the hearths of the house during the Civil War.

Chapter Forty-one

Early Norfolk Baptist Highlights

Freemason Street Baptist Church is the oldest existing Baptist house of worship in Norfolk.

An outgrowth of Cumberland Street Baptist Church and a lineal descendant of Norfolk's first racially mixed Baptist congregation that met during the early 1800s in the temporarily abandoned Borough Church, now St. Paul's Episcopal Church, the Freemason Street congregation was organized on May 25, 1848.

The story behind its origin is an interesting commentary on human frailty.

The minister of Cumberland Street Baptist Church was indiscreet enough to become engaged to two young women at the same time. And when he decided to favor one and slighted the other, a rift occurred in his congregation. Although the majority of his flock gave him a vote of confidence, eighty members decided to withdraw and establish a church of their own.

And since Thomas U. Walter, the celebrated Philadelphia architect who later designed the dome of the Capitol in Washington, was in Norfolk acting as a consultant on the Norfolk Court House then under construction, he was asked to provide a plan for the new church.

A good Baptist, Walter obliged, and the cornerstone was laid on August 14, 1848. Two years later, on May 30, 1850, the new church was dedicated. The Rev. Tiberius Gracchus Jones, one of the great figures in Virginia Baptist history, was its first minister.

The tall steeple of the church holds aloft the only one left of the dozens of plain and fancy old weathervanes that formerly indicated the direction of the wind in downtown Norfolk. Created by some long-forgotten Nineteenth Century tinsmith, the vane is an imaginative copy of Gabriel's trumpet. It was placed on top of the original spire (a much taller one than the present one) when the church was built.

According to tradition, a prominent Presbyterian who lived directly opposite the church objected strenuously to the original steeple because he was afraid that it might topple in a high wind and crash on his house. He was finally talked out of his objection, however, by a Baptist acquaintance who assured him that "The devil would hardly look for a good Presbyterian under a Baptist steeple."

The first Freemason Street steeple was the tallest structure in Norfolk from 1850 until it was blown down in the great August storm of 1879 that hit Norfolk on the morning of August 18. When it was over, half of the houses in the Norfolk area were roofless, and hundreds of trees were uprooted. At the height of the storm a reporter from The Norfolk Virginian, who was out checking on the damage, passed a woman in a doorway and heard her give a terrified shriek. When he asked what was wrong, she screamed, "My God, the Baptist steeple has blown down on all those houses!"

Fortunately she was wrong, for the steeple fell into Freemason Street instead. And when the debris was cleared away the weathervane was found thrust upright in the ground a considerable distance from the church.

At that time, many of those who were familiar with its appearance high in the air flocked to inspect it at closer range, and it was found to be so large that a tall man could stand upright in the larger end of the tin horn.

But the Freemason Street Baptists had to have their steeple, and when it was replaced with the present one, the trumpet weathervane was again placed on its top, where it continues to revolve with every passing breeze.

Chapter Forty-two

Forrest—Norfolk's First Historian

Norfolk history buffs owe a great deal to William H. Forrest, the author of the first serious historical work on the Norfolk area.

Although Forrest's prose style is a trifle rococo for contemporary tastes, his historical writings preserve a gold mine of out-of-the-way information concerning the Norfolk area that would have been forgotten if he had not had the foresight to set it down.

Forrest was born near London Bridge in Princess Anne County (now the City of Virginia Beach) in 1817. He was a son of John P. C. and Mrs. Elizabeth Forrest. Not too much is known concerning his earlier years, but he was always interested in his adpoted city and was known as one of its most progressive citizens.

When he was thirty, he began a weekly paper in Norfolk called the Virginia Temperance Advocate. The first issue, dated May 15, 1847, stated that it was dedicated to "temperance, morality, literature, health, etc."

Feeling the great need for a city directory, there having been none since 1806-07, Forrest set about compiling a systematic listing of the inhabitants of the city and its many growing businesses. The directory, published in 1851-52, lists him as "William S. Forrest, editor and proprietor of the Norfolk Directory, No. 6 South Brewer St., near Freemason."

While compiling the directory, Forrest felt the necessity of a good general history of Norfolk and its vicinity. His "Historical and Descriptive Sketches of Norfolk and Vicinity. . . . During a Period of 200 Years" was published in 1853 and was an immediate success.

Forrest was blessed with an excellent memory and the knack of never forgetting intimate details concerning persons and important happenings. He also had access to many private papers and files of old newspapers that no longer exist, and his extracts from them have proved invaluable to latter-day historians.

Norfolk had a population of sixteen thousand at the time the history was issued. Two years later, the city was almost wiped out by the worst yellow fever epidemic in its history. Fortunately, Forrest survived the disaster and incorporated his observations in "The Great Pestilence in Virginia," which was published a year after the epidemic.

This volume is one of the best accounts of the terrible summer of 1855, when the only vessel to enter the harbor was a small steamer transporting mail and coffins from the Washington and Richmond steamers anchored in Hampton Roads.

Throughout this period, Forrest was also connected with The Daily Southern Argus and Virginia and North Carolina Advertiser. This was the Norfolk "states' rights" paper of the period and was dedicated to "Southern Views and Southern Rights."

The Argus was discontinued in 1861 after almost every man in its plant had joined the Confederate Army. Forrest was the "local editor," or what would today be known as the "city editor," of the Argus.

After the Civil War, Forrest entered the real estate business. He was a great promoter of railroads coming into the Norfolk area and was particularly interested in making Norfolk the port for the Eastern North Carolina trade.

He died on October 10, 1878, and was buried in Elmwood

Cemetery. His funeral took place at Cumberland Street Methodist Church, which was torn down a few years ago to provide additional parking space for the congregation of St. Paul's Episcopal Church.

Chapter Forty-three

Norfolk and the Navy

Norfolk has always been a Navy town, a tradition it is likely to maintain as long as men go down to the sea in ships.

From the time of the founding of the town in the late Seventeenth Century, an ever-increasing commerce necessitated the establishing and maintaining of taverns and boarding houses along the waterfront to accommodate the captains and crews of vessels between voyages. And the nearness of Norfolk to the sea soon made its harbor a favorite rendezvous for foreign men-of-war.

This is evident from the recollections of Mrs. Helen Calvert Maxwell Read, whose father, Maximilian Calvert, was mayor of Norfolk in 1765 and 1769.

In her old age, Mrs. Read liked to recall how the visit of thirty-two midshipmen from a fifty-gun British ship, "mostly boys and lads of good families, and several of them sprigs of nobility," set the hearts of Norfolk damsels aflutter.

But the picture also had its darker side; and throughout most of its history, Norfolk has also been troubled occasionally by serious riots caused by sailormen.

In the main, however, Norfolk's nautical history has been glamorous.

Two famous Nineteenth Century expeditions set out from Norfolk-area waters to make world history. In August of 1838, the first national exploratory expedition authorized under a special act of Congress, known as the Wilkes Expedition, left Norfolk for a four-year cruise to survey and chart areas in the Pacific Ocean and the South Seas, particularly those parts most frequently used by American whaling vessels. On November 24, 1852, Commodore Matthew Calbraith Perry left Norfolk on the paddle frigate Mississippi, the nucleus of the "Japan Squadron" that resulted in the opening of the ports of Japan to the United States two years later.

Over the years Norfolk has been the scene of thousands of marriages between seagoing men and Norfolk girls, giving the city, among others, the nickname "The Mother-in-Law of the Navy." Notable among these was the marriage of Commodore Stephen Decatur and Miss Susan Wheeler, which took place on March 8, 1806, and the two marriages of Admiral David Glasgow Farragut.

Farragut's first marriage to Miss Susan Caroline Marchant of Norfolk took place on September 1, 1824. After her death he married another Norfolk girl, Miss Virginia D. Loyall, on December 26, 1843.

But Farragut had other Norfolk connections.

Early in 1811, the ten-year-old lad, who was already a midshipman, had a memorable encounter on the Norfolk waterfront that has become a part of naval history.

When the gig of the man-of-war Essex, commanded by Captain David Porter, was standing by at a Norfolk wharf awaiting the return of Porter from some business ashore, a crowd of dock loafers began making fun of the bantam midshipman. Young Farragut faced his tormentors in silence until one of them began sprinkling him with a watering pot "to make him grow."

Quick as a flash, Farragut snagged the fellow with his boat hook and yanked him down into the gig. The sailors, idling at their oars, were spoiling for a fight, and this was their signal.

Led by Farragut, who brandished a dirk, they leaped from the boat and drove the hecklers up what was then known as Market Square, later as Commercial Place. Minutes later, the law took over, and Farragut, his companions, and his tormentors were taken before a justice, who bound them over to keep the public peace.

When Captain Porter heard of the affair, however, he was delighted at his protege's prowess and praised him for being "three pounds of uniform and seventy pounds of fight."

Chapter Forty-four

Norfolk's Civil War Phase

The storm clouds of the Civil War began to gather over Norfolk as early as November 10, 1860, when the Daily Southern Argus, the city's "states' rights" paper editorialized:

"Sooner or later the ties which now link together the North and South must be sundered. How closely the inevitable effect will follow the cause, may be a matter of speculation, but it can only be a matter of time. When those shall govern the confederacy who pronounce Southern life utter 'barbarism,' and denounce as 'the sum of all villanies' a practice on which our whole section sustains itself, the South must secede if secession is practicable."

But there were those in Norfolk who felt otherwise. A correspondent to the Herald and Norfolk and Portsmouth Advertiser suggested that Virginia cast her lot with the North rather than the cotton states. "Their slave property," he wrote, "both by the duty and policy of the free States, would be secured, until it could be gotten rid of by gradual sales. There would be, on the part of the free States, a cordial and sincere co-operation in this scheme."

Such were the two schools of thought in Norfolk on the eve of the war. But as time passed, the more radical Southern attitude prevailed.

On December 20, 1860, when South Carolina seceded from the Union, the Herald, strongly Unionist in sentiment, asked why Virginia should "dance crazily out of the Union to the fiddling of South Carolina?"

But the Argus applauded the act by trumpeting, "Right nobly the proud and brave sons of South Carolina met the emergency. At one stroke they have severed the chains which bind them to a tyrannous North, and they now stand before the world an independent people."

South Carolina's move was followed in rapid succession by Mississippi, Florida, Alabama, Georgia, Louisiana, and Texas. Finally, when President Lincoln called for volunteers to put down the rebellion, Virginia voted to secede from the Union on April 17, 1861.

Prior to this, Southern sentiment was rapidly gaining the upper hand in Norfolk, and one impatient citizen had already unfurled the Confederate flag, with its seven stars encircling the letters "Va.," from the roof of a house on Wolfe, now Market, Street on April 2, 1861. This was followed on April 12, 1861 by a party of young enthusiasts who sailed down the river to Craney Island and hoisted the same colors over the old blockhouse there.

With the secession of Virginia, followed rapidly by Arkansas, North Carolina, and Tennessee, the die was cast and life in Norfolk marched to a quicker pace as its citizens prepared for war. From then on, Norfolk's Confederate history blazed bravely, if briefly.

At 3:20 a.m. on April 21, 1861, the Gosport Navy Yard containing millions of dollars of naval stores and arms, together with several naval vessels moored in the Elizabeth River, were put to the torch by the evacuating Federal forces. According to one contemporary account, "The scene was grand and terrific beyond description. The roar of the conflagration was loud enough to be heard at three or four miles distance, and to this were added occasional discharges from the heavy guns of the old Pennsylvania."

One of the vessels that was partially burned was the new steam frigate, the USS Merrimack, then regarded as the "Queen of the Navy." What was left of her was later converted into the CSS Virginia that locked horns with the USS Monitor on March 9, 1862, in the first battle between ironclads, the grand finale of Norfolk's Confederate phase.

On May 10, 1862, Federal forces recaptured Norfolk, the Merrimack was scuttled and blown up by her crew early the next morning, and the United States flag again flapped atop the Corinthian portico of the Customs House on Main Street.

Chapter Forty-five

Virginia's First Civil War Engagement

Contrary to popular belief, the first Battle of Manassas (July 21, 1861) was not the first engagement fought in Virginia during the Civil War.

The first skirmish, the little known Battle of Sewells Point, was fought on May 18-19, 1861, on ground now occupied by the Norfolk Naval Station.

The events leading up to the initial engagement on Virginia soil had moved with whirlwind rapidity.

On December 20, 1860, South Carolina became the first state to secede from the Union. Four months later, on April 12, 1861, troops of the same state opened fire on Fort Sumter in Charleston harbor, bringing a quick request from President Lincoln for volunteers to march against the rebelling states.

Five days later, Virginia became the eighth Southern state to withdraw from the Union. And on April 21, 1861, the Gosport Navy Yard (now the Norfolk Naval Shipyard) was abandoned and partially burned by the Federal forces, leaving only Fort Monroe at Old Point Comfort as the last bastion of the United States in Tidewater Virginia.

Stewart's "History of Norfolk County, Virginia" (1902), contains a detailed account of the Battle of Sewells Point that took place one month later. Shorn of unnecessary details, this is what happened:

On May 18, 1861, Norfolk-area and Georgia Confederate troops began erecting land batteries at Sewells Point opposite Fort Monroe on Hampton Roads.

By 5 o'clock that evening, three guns and two rifled guns had been mounted and work was rapidly progressing on the fortifications when the USS Monticello, commanded by Captain Henry Eagle, steamed over from Fort Monroe to see what was afoot.

Not liking what he saw, Captain Eagle gave the order to open fire. One of the shots from his vessel hit the battery, throwing turf high in the air.

In the meantime, the Monticello had been joined by an armed tug, also from Fort Monroe.

The bombardment from these two vessels caused momentary confusion in the breastworks, but once the Confederates had recovered from the initial shock, immediate preparations were made to return the fire from their two 32-pounders and the two rifled guns already in position.

In the absence of a Confederate or Virginia flag, Captain Peyton H. Colquitt of the Light Guard of Columbus, Georgia, who was in charge of the erection of the battery, called for the raising of the Georgia flag on the Sewells Point ramparts.

Under the cover of darkness, the armed tug returned to Fort Monroe, but the Monticello remained off Sewells Point with her guns pointed in the direction of the Confederate fortifications.

During the night, frantic efforts were made to complete the breastworks, and it was not until the next day at around 5:50 in the afternoon, when the sound of axes being used to secure the Confederate gun carriages could be plainly heard aboard the Monticello, that the bombardment was resumed. It continued until 6:45 p.m.

In the end, the Monticello, with several gaping holes in her hull from well-aimed Confederate shots, limped back to Fort Monroe. The first engagement on Virginia soil during the Civil War was over.

There were no fatalities on either side. The only person wounded was Confederate Private Alexander Sykes of the Wise Light Dragoons, who was struck by a fragment of a bursting shell.

Subsequently the Sewells Point batteries were under fire many times, but they were never silenced or captured in combat. And when Norfolk was evacuated by the Confederate forces on May 10, 1862, they were abandoned.

Chapter Forty-six

Lincoln Plans the Recapture of Norfolk

Abraham Lincoln never set foot in Norfolk, but he visited the area briefly in 1862 and helped plan the campaign that resulted in taking the city from the Confederate forces.

McClellan's army was in the first stages of the Peninsula campaign, and the CSS Virginia (the former USS Merrimack) and the Monitor had just locked horns on March 9, 1862, in Hampton Roads. At that point, Lincoln decided to visit Fort Monroe, "to ascertain by personal observation whether some further vigilance and vigor might not be infused into the operation of the Army and Navy."

As the presidential party, consisting of Lincoln, Secretary

of State Salmon P. Chase, Secretary of War Edwin M. Stanton, and Brigadier General Egbert Ludovickus Viele left Washington on May 5, 1862, news arrived that the Confederate forces had withdrawn from Yorktown. The trip down the bay on the Coast Guard cutter Miami was rough and it was not until around nine o'clock the next night that Fort Monroe was reached.

After an early breakfast, the presidential party visited the Monitor and then went over to the Rip Raps. Just then the Virginia steamed into sight off Sewells Point, and as it was surmised that she might again engage the Monitor, the party took time off to see a fight that never took place.

That night it was decided that Norfolk must be captured in order to deprive the Virginia of her supply base. And the next morning a bombardment of the Sewells Point batteries was begun. But the sudden appearance of the Virginia put an end to the attack. It was then realized that a successful landing could only be made on the south side of Hampton Roads in a spot out of range of the Virginia's guns. And on May 9, 1862, Secretary Chase, Gen. John E. Wool, and others conducted a reconnaissance operation off Ocean View.

Returning to Fort Monroe, they found Lincoln in consultation with a pilot familiar with Norfolk area waters. The party then set out again, this time including Lincoln, who refused to permit an attack on Confederates that could easily be seen on the beach. That night, six thousand troops were ferried across to Ocean View on the Old Bay Line steamer Adelaide. No resistance was made. In the meantime, panic reigned in Norfolk where the Confederate forces, under General Benjamin Huger, were preparing to evacuate the city and burn the Gosport Navy Yard.

Lincoln, Chase, Stanton, and General Wool came over to Ocean View early the next morning but found that the troops had already begun their march toward Norfolk. Chase and Wool followed them, but Lincoln and Stanton returned to Fort Monroe to await the results. Little resistance was encountered by the troops, but upon reaching Indian Pole Bridge (now the site of the Granby Street Bridge), they found that it had been fired by the retreating Confederates and a detour had to be made.

Mayor William Wilson Lamb and other members of the Norfolk Council were awaiting them on Princess Anne Road with a flag of truce, and General Wool accepted the surrender of the city and rode back into Norfolk with Mayor Lamb and Secretary Chase in the mayor's carriage.

After Mayor Lamb had explained the surrender to a crowd at the Court House, three cheers were given for Jefferson Davis and three groans for Lincoln. Later that evening, when General Wool and Secretary Chase returned to Fort Monroe, they went straight to Lincoln's room.

"Norfolk is ours!" Wool announced. Stanton was so delighted with the news that he hugged the general. The next morning as the presidential party was about to embark on the USS Baltimore to return to Washington, Commodore Louis M. Goldsborough announced that the Virginia had been blown up by her men off Craney Island. Lincoln then visited Norfolk's inner harbor to see the still-burning Navy Yard. Anchoring off Norfolk, he and his party discovered that the Monitor and other United States vessels had preceded them.

After a brief stop at Fort Monroe, the Baltimore proceeded back to Washington. In the words of Secretary Chase, "So ended a brilliant week's campaign by the President."

Chapter Forty-seven

The Hanging of Dr. Wright

The hanging of Dr. David Minton Wright for the murder of Federal Lieutenant A. L. Sanborn was a grisly highlight of the Norfolk Civil War period.

Born in 1812 in Nansemond County, Dr. Wright moved to Norfolk in 1853 from Edenton, N. C., where he had married

Miss Penelope Creecy. In 1855, when the Norfolk area was prostrated by the worst yellow fever epidemic in its history, Dr. Wright was stricken. He recovered, however, and his unselfish attentions to the sick and dying of his adopted city won him the respect of everyone.

Although a Southerner, Dr. Wright was a Unionist and opposed Virginia's secession from the Union. Once that took place, he remained in Norfolk.

On June 17, 1863, a little over a year after Norfolk was retaken by the Federal forces, Dr. Wright was walking west on Main Street from a celebration of his wedding anniversary. Arriving at Church and Main streets, he met a column of Negro Federal soldiers under the command of a white lieutenant, A. L. Sanborn.

Resentment in Norfolk was then running high against the presence of Negro troops, and as Dr. Wright shared that feeling, he approached Sanborn with clenched fists, saying, "Oh! You coward!"

Sanborn halted his troops, turned to Wright, and said, "You are under arrest." At that point the soldiers moved in to apprehend him. Maddened at the thought of being seized by the Negro soldiers, the doctor did a rash thing, two versions of which have been reported. One says he pulled a pistol from an inner coat pocket and fired twice at Sanborn. The other says the pistol was handed to him by a spectator. Be that as it may, Sanborn was wounded, staggered into Foster & Moore's Drug Store, and died, after which Wright was arrested and charged with murder.

During his trial, his admirers stood outside the courtroom and lifted their hats silently as he hobbled in and out, his wrists and ankles heavily chained.

Wright was found guilty and was sentenced to be hanged, a verdict that Norfolk people resented as they regarded him as a martyr to the Southern cause. Powerful influences were brought to bear to save his life, but all of them failed.

In the meantime the doctor's daughter, Penelope, decided to do something to save her father. Visiting him in his dimly lighted cell, she exchanged her outer clothing with him, slipped on his boots, and crept under the blankets of his cot. The doctor then walked out of his cell and had gone fifty yards from the door of the prison to a waiting carriage when a sharp-eyed sentry called attention to his unusual height and masculine gait. Wright was then recaptured, but his daughter was not detained or molested.

As the time for the execution drew near, President Lincoln granted a week's reprieve in order to give the case more study, but in the end he refused to intervene.

Wright was taken to the scaffold set up in the center of a racetrack on the outskirts of the city on October 23, 1863 between long columns of troops, while the sound of wailing was heard from shuttered houses all along the way. Troops were posted in a square around the gallows, while thousands of spectators looked on from rooftops or stood on tiptoe in wagons, carts and buggies.

Wright had made his own coffin of cypress wood while he was in prison, and after his body had been turned over to his family, it was placed in it and taken to Old Christ Church for the funeral. Inside the lid of the coffin were pictures of the doctor's wife and children, one of them his oldest son, who had been killed three months earlier at the Battle of Gettysburg.

But the doctor never knew that his son had died for the cause that he had disapproved of at the beginning of the war. When the news of the young man's death was learned, the family spared him and never told him the sad news.

Chapter Forty-eight

A Norfolk Girl Told President Davis

Contrary to the well-known story told for years by the little old lady who was a guide in Richmond's historic St. Paul's

Episcopal Church, a courier from General Robert E. Lee was not the first person to notify Confederate President Jefferson Davis that Richmond had to be evacuated.

Miss Elizabeth Selden (Bettie) Saunders, the fiancee of Norfolk-born Colonel Walter Herron Taylor, Lee's aide-de-camp, was, according to a well-authenticated tradition handed down in her family, the first person to give President Davis the bad news.

Miss Saunders, a daughter of United States Navy Captain John L. Saunders and Mrs. Martha Bland Selden Saunders, lived during the war with the family of Lewis D. Crenshaw in Richmond, where she worked in the Confederate Mint and the Confederate Medical Department.

It was to the Crenshaw house that Colonel Taylor, to whom she was engaged, sent a special messenger either on Saturday night, April 1, 1865, or on early Sunday morning, April 2, to notify her that the Confederate capital had to be evacuated.

Colonel Taylor had instructed his fiancee to go as soon as possible to St. Paul's Episcopal Church and ask the rector to be at the Crenshaw house Sunday night at midnight to perform the marriage ceremony.

Before sending the messenger, Colonel Taylor had received special permission from General Lee to go to Richmond to give Miss Saunders "the protection of his name."

Miss Saunders went to the church just before the morning service was about to begin and met Dr. Charles Minnigerode, the rector, on the church portico. While she was talking to him, President Davis arrived for Morning Prayer. Overhearing the conversation, Davis asked for more details. And according to the story as it has been handed down in the Taylor family, Miss Saunders told him, "Walter would hardly have bothered to send a special messenger to me if conditions didn't warrant it."

Davis, greatly disturbed by the news, went into the church and took his seat in the Presidential Pew. A few minutes later, General Lee's official courier walked down the asile and whispered to Davis, who arose and left abruptly.

That night after midnight, on April 3, 1865, while the evacuating Confederates fired the city and looters ran wild in its streets, Colonel Taylor and Miss Bettie Saunders were married in the parlor of the Crenshaw house. Because of wartime inflation, the bride's wedding shoes cost three hundred dollars.

High water brought on by the spring rains, and poor rail connections, had almost prevented the groom from arriving on time for the ceremony. Afterward, Lewis Crenshaw accompanied Colonel Taylor as far back toward the Confederate lines as safety permitted.

One week after Appomattox, Colonel Taylor returned to Richmond, picked up his bride, and drove her back to Norfolk in a buggy.

Chapter Forty-nine

Norfolk's Two Civil War Monuments

Norfolk has two Civil War monuments — the well-known Confederate Monument re-erected early in 1971 near its original site adjacent to the soaring Virginia National Bank in the downtown area, and the lesser-known memorial shaft dedicated to Negro Civil War Army and Navy veterans that dominates West Point Cemetery adjoining Elmwood Cemetery north of Princess Anne Road.

Long-cherished hopes of erecting a Confederate monument in Norfolk became a reality early in 1898 when sufficient funds had been raised to make it possible.

On January 28, 1898, permission was granted by the City of Norfolk to use the space at the head of Commercial Place (earlier known as Market Square) on which it was erected. And on February 22, 1899, the cornerstone was laid on the thirty-second anniversary of the inauguration of Jefferson Davis as president of the Confederacy.

The monument was designed by the Couper Marble Works of Norfolk. The original plan called for it to be topped with a heroic bronze figure of Peace, while four life-sized bronze figures representing a Confederate sailor, infantryman, cavalryman, and artilleryman were intended to adorn the base. But money was scarce, and the committee finally settled for a handsome fifteen-foot bronze statue of a defiant Johnny Reb by Norfolk-born sculptor William Couper as the crowning feature of the monument that was unveiled on May 16, 1907.

Originally a focal point in the downtown area, the monument was a symbol in bronze and stone of the Lost Cause. But eventually the tides of progress abandoned it, and in 1924 a proposal was made to move it to another location.

This caused a resounding chorus of rebel yells, notable among them the hue and cry raised by the late Mrs. Frank Anthony Walke, popularly known as "Mrs. Confederacy." With fire in her eyes, Mrs. Walke defied the city fathers so effectively that they dropped the matter like a hot potato, or rather a hot minie ball. In June of 1954, the matter was again broached, at which time Norfolk Mayor W. Fred Duckworth aroused the ire of the United Daughters of the Confederacy when he referred to the monument as a "glorified pigeon roost." But it was not until 1964-65 that the monument was finally taken down for fear that it would be damaged by the pile drivers preparing the foundations for the Virginia National Bank Building.

Cleaned and re-erected six years later, the monument now provides a pleasing contrast to the functional architecture that surrounds it.

James E. Fuller (1846-1909) of Norfolk, a former slave and a former quartermaster in the First United States Colored Cavalry, was the motivating spirit behind the erection of

Norfolk's Negro Civil War Memorial. An employee of the Norfolk Customs House, Fuller was largely responsible for the City Council's granting of a portion of the West Point Cemetery in 1886 as a special burial place for Negro Union veterans.

Depending on chicken pot pie suppers, raffles, and concerts to raise funds, the committee headed by Fuller finally had enough money to begin the monument in 1906. The cornerstone was laid on Decoration Day the same year. Completed in 1920, the monument is topped by a brown metal statue of a Negro Union private wearing a kepi, a tightly buttoned tunic, a shoulder strap bearing the initials "U.S.A.," ribbed stockings, and heavy shoes.

Backed by a simulated wooden stump, the figure holds a regulation Civil War rifle and has a replica of a bayonet attached to his belt.

White marble plaques inserted in the monument's base record the names of the Grand Army of the Republic camps and other Negro groups which contributed to the memorial's completion.

Chapter Fifty

Norfolk's Early Jewish History

Norfolk's Jewish history dates from 1787, the year Moses Myers (1753-1835), the builder of the elegant Myers House at the corner of Freemason and Bank streets and Norfolk's first known permanent Jewish citizen, arrived in the borough.

Myers, who according to Norfolk-born historian Hugh Blair Grigsby, was the last gentleman in the borough to wear his hair in the Eighteenth Century fashion with a ribbon-tied queue at the nape of his neck, was followed by other Jews, most of them merchants or small shopkeepers.

Although there was no regular synagogue in the Norfolk of that period, it is possible, according to Dr. Malcolm H. Stern, the Jewish historian and a former rabbi of Norfolk's

Ohef Sholom Temple, that the Norfolk Jewish community had grown sufficiently by 1815 to provide the required ten adult males needed for Jewish worship. Dr. Stern's assumption is based on the recorded discovery in 1840 of several Torahs in a house known as "The Castle" on Cumberland street.

By 1820, Norfolk area Jews were sufficiently numerous to establish a cemetery of their own on a lot purchased for that purpose in what is now Berkley. By 1850, however, Norfolk's Jewish population, which had been greatly augmented by the wave of German Jewish immigration to the United States, had increased so rapidly that the present Hebrew Cemetery at Tidewater Drive and Princess Anne Road was established. At that time many of the bodies and tombstones of those who had been buried in the Berkley cemetery were moved to the new location.

The first actual records of Jewish worship in Norfolk date from 1844, when Jacob Umstadter, a newly arrived Orthodox German Jew, agreed to become the schochet (Kosher butcher) and hazan (Cantor) of the Norfolk Jewish community.

By 1848, the community had grown sufficiently to permit the organization of a regular congregation. Two rooms were rented in the home of Nathan American, one of the members, for the conducting of regular worship services, and Aaron L. Goldsmith, another member, was sent to Baltimore to purchase a Torah.

Norfolk's first Jewish congregation assumed the name Chevra B'nai Jacov, literally "Association of the Sons of Jacob," or, as they translated it, "House of Jacob."

Continued growth caused the congregation to move into the first floor of the former Norfolk Lyceum, then the Odd Fellows Hall on Wolfe (later Market) Street. It remained there until February of 1859, when the building was destroyed by fire. This caused a temporary removal to quarters at 137 South Church Street.

102

By that time, members of the House of Jacob had begun to think in terms of erecting a regular synagogue, and on March 3, 1859, they purchased a lot on the east side of Cumberland Street opposite the Old Norfolk Academy from Jacob and Fanny Umstadter. On that site, John M. Sale, a Norfolk builder, erected Norfolk's first Jewish synagogue, a Victorian Gothic structure.

When it was completed, according to Dr. Stern, "Mr. Umstadter, who apparently trusted no one but his Maker, took the trouble to record the purchase of his synagogue seats in the Deeds of the Norfolk Corporation Court."

Until the arrival of the first ordained rabbi, Bernard L. Fould, there was no regular rabbi, and capable members of the congregation, all of them foreign born and most of German origin, conducted the services in Orthodox chanting fashion.

The Civil War, according to Dr. Stern, brought with it a sweep of liberalism in American Jewish life which penetrated the Norfolk Jewish community.

In 1867, when the congregation was reorganized under the name of Ohef Sholom, "Lovers of Peace," ideological differences appeared within the synagogue.

In 1870, the more traditional faction withdrew from the congregation and formed what is today Beth El Temple. The Ohef Sholom, or more liberal group, was the progenitor of today's Ohef Sholom Temple at Raleigh Avenue and Stockley Gardens.

Chapter Fifty-one

The Old Bells of Norfolk

Like their counterparts all over the country, the old bells of Norfolk once performed the important tasks of calling the faithful to worship, sounding distress alarms, tolling for calamities, or voicing exultation in times of civic or national rejoicing.

Now, with the exception of a few isolated examples, they are either mute or have been replaced by electronic devices that are poor substitutes for their pleasantly resounding peals.

What is believed to be the oldest church bell in Norfolk is in Christ and St. Luke's Episcopal Church at Olney Road and Stockley Gardens. This venerable tocsin was moved to its present position in the tall granite Gothic tower of the church from the steeple of Old Christ Church at Freemason and Cumberland streets in 1909.

The bell is inscribed "Christ Church" and weighs 1,218 pounds. It is forty-two inches in diameter, has "G" tone, and is provided with two clappers, one for tolling and one for ringing. It is rung by hand for the regular church services and is also tolled for funerals, a special device attached to the bell for the latter making it sound suitably mournful.

The Christ Church bell was cast in 1860 by the Meneely Bell Foundry in West Troy, N. Y., and replaced the original church bell dating from 1829. The latter was cracked in 1859, at which time it was part of the Norfolk City Clock that had been in the belfry of Old Christ Church since 1829. The second bell, the one now in use, was incorporated in the clock system to replace the original bell and remained in use there until Christ and St. Luke's was built, at which time it was transferred to its present place and the clock was given to the College of William and Mary in Williamsburg.

As far as is known, the first church in Norfolk to have a bell was the so-called "Bell Church," Norfolk's first Presbyterian church, erected in 1802 at Catharine (now Bank) and Charlotte streets. It is not known what happened to the bell that gave the church its name. Norfolk's second Presbyterian church was across the street from the present St. Paul's Episcopal Church. Originally it did not have a belfry, but around 1860, when it was restyled in the Gothic manner, a belfry was built and a bell was bought for it. But it was never hung.

At the outbreak of the Civil War, it was presented to the

Confederate government to be melted down for military purposes. But the Yankees beat the Rebels to the draw. According to a letter received in Norfolk many years later, a native of Boston remembered seeing this bell carted through the streets of that city, bearing the placard, "This bell was captured from the Presbyterian Church in Norfolk, Va." The letter also added the fact that the bell wound up in the tower of a ferry house.

Two other old Norfolk bells deserve mention.

The bell of St. Mary's Catholic Church at Holt and Chapel Streets was cast in 1884 by the McShane Bell Foundry of Baltimore. It is forty-two inches in diameter, weighs 1,500 pounds, and is of "G" tone. It is still rung by hand to announce masses on Sunday and holy days of obligation, and it is also tolled for funerals. According to the centennial history of St. Mary's, published in 1958, the clock and bell of the church were supported at one time by public funds as a means by which Norfolkians of that neighborhood could regulate their daily activities.

The other bell is the Norfolk jail bell, currently perched on top of the motorcycle garage of the Public Safety Building. Inscribed "Joshua Register, Baltimore 1867," this old tocsin replaced an earlier one cast during the 1850s for the Gothic style Norfolk City Jail that was built during the same period on Avon Street behind the Norfolk City Hall and Court House, now the MacArthur Memorial.

The original bell, metal from which is incorporated in the present one, was cracked on January 1, 1863, when it was being rung to celebrate the Emancipation Proclamation.

Chapter Fifty-two

Other Distinguished Visitors

Although Norfolk put out the welcome mat for Lafayette in 1824-25 and General Robert E. Lee in 1870, they were not the only famous visitors to the borough and city in its early history.

Leading the list was Benjamin Franklin, who, as deputy postmaster of the colonies, visited Williamsburg on official business in 1756. Returning to Philadelphia by the way of Norfolk, he was made an honorary citizen of the borough on April 10, 1756.

George Washington was next. He visited Norfolk briefly in May 1763 while he was on an inspection trip to his lands in the Dismal Swamp. Thirteen years later, John Marshall, later chief justice of the United States, was in Norfolk for a short time after having taken part in the Battle of Great Bridge on December 9, 1775.

Thomas Jefferson arrived next, by ship, on November 29, 1789. He and his two daughters, Martha and Mary, were returning from France, where he had been United States minister since 1785. Mary, at least, did not like Norfolk, for the French-educated young lady burst into tears upon catching sight of the borough, sobbing, "Mais c'est bien different de Paris (But this is very different from Paris)."

Jefferson was followed by Thomas Moore, the Irish poet, in 1803-04. Moore didn't like Norfolk either, calling it a "disagreeable place," adding, "It abounds in dogs, in Negroes, and in Democrats."

James Monroe was Norfolk's next distinguished guest, paying the borough two visits during his two-term administration. The first was in 1818 during the celebration of the opening of the Dismal Swamp Canal. The second was a year later for the laying of the cornerstone of the United States Customs House at Wide Water and Church Streets.

The eccentric John Randolph of Roanoke came next. He came to Norfolk to meet the USS Concord, which took him across the Atlantic as United States ambassador to Russia. While he was in Norfolk he was entertained at an elaborate banquet at the

Exchange Hotel on Main Street on June 26, 1830.

The famous Indian chief, Black Hawk, and several of his warriors came next and created great excitement. They arrived in Norfolk on June 2, 1833, and were quartered in the Exchange Hotel. They were taken to visit the Gosport Navy Yard, where they were delighted with the 74-gun USS Delaware, which they dubbed a "great canoe."

Prince Louis Napoleon, later the Emperor Napoleon III, arrived in April, 1837, on board the French frigate L'Andromede, He was the first guest to register at French's Hotel at Main and Church streets and was described as "a fine looking man, erect, dignified and masculine in person, but not resembling in features his late, great uncle."

Henry Clay next electrified Norfolk with his oratory in a two-day visit on April 24-25, 1844. He was followed by Edgar Allan Poe, who delivered his lecture, "The Poetic Principle," on September 16, 1849, in the Old Norfolk Academy on Bank Street. It was to be Poe's last public appearance before his tragic death in Baltimore one month later. Earlier in the century, Poe visited Norfolk in the company of his mother, Mrs. Elizabeth Arnold Poe, an actress.

On April 24, 1850, General Winfield Scott (Old Fuss and Feathers), the hero of the Mexican War, was entertained in Norfolk. Scott had also served earlier in Norfolk as a captain of a military company from Petersburg during the War of 1812.

President Millard Filmore came for a visit in 1851 and was followed on August 25, 1860, by Stephen A. Douglas (The Little Giant), who spoke to a crowd of more than five thousand from the portico of the Norfolk Court House (now the MacArthur Memorial). In recalling the event, John S. Wise, in "The End of an Era" (1899), said: "I drove into Norfolk, and seeing a great crowd assembled, paused and heard part of a speech by Stephen A. Douglas. I was greatly impressed by his tremendous voice, every tone of which reached me more than a block away."

Chapter Fifty-three

Education in Old Norfolk

Although a lot on the east side of "the street that leadest into the woods," that later became Church Street and is now St. Paul's Boulevard, was provided for a schoolhouse by the Lower Norfolk County authorities when Norfolk was laid out in 1680-81, there was no school building on the property until around 1761.

In the intervening eighty years there were four ways a child could learn his "three R's" in the borough.

Well-to-do citizens provided private tutors for their children; a parish school for boys was conducted off and on by the ministers or parish clerks of Elizabeth River Parish; an enterprising lad could be apprenticed to a merchant to learn arithmetic, spelling, bookkeeping and how to write a legible hand from a senior mercantile clerk; or a girl could obtain the rudiments of an education, "needlework, and marking on a sampler" by attending what was then known as a "Dame's School," usually operated in their own homes by literate but impecunious widows or spinsters.

The first step toward organized public education in the borough was taken in 1728, when Samuel Boush I and Thomas Newton, acting as trustees for the Norfolk County Court for unsold public lands in the town, conveyed half of the lot originally set aside in 1680-81 for a school to Samuel Boush II, Nathaniel Newton, and Samuel Smith who agreed to erect a schoolhouse on the property and to employ a master. As nothing was done, however, the Virginia General Assembly took matters into its hands in 1752 and authorized the Norfolk County Court and the Norfolk Borough Council jointly to hire a schoolmaster and establish a Grammar School on the still vacant schoolhouse lot.

As this produced no action, the Assembly passed a new act

in 1762, vesting the sole control of the proposed Grammar School in the borough council. This act, passed in March 1762, states, ". . . a schoolhouse hath been built on the said lot . . ." As far as can be determined now, this was the first schoolhouse erected for that purpose in the borough. This was the beginning of the present Norfolk Academy.

As this building presumably was destroyed at the beginning of the Revolutionary War when Norfolk was burned by the British and Virginia forces, the aldermen and common council of the borough appointed commissioners on December 6, 1785, to ". . . agree with some person or persons to rebuild the free school . . ." The rebuilt school, known for the first time as the "Norfolk Academy" and headed by the Reverend Walker Maury, opened in 1786, at which time it ceased to be a free school, a tuition fee being charged.

Its curriculum consisted of reading, writing, arithmetic, bookkeeping, English grammar, geography and the use of the globes, and Latin, Greek, and French. Pupils of the first class were distinguished by a broad black ribbon thrown over the right shoulder and under the left, while those in the lower grades wore a blue ribbon in the buttonholes of their coats.

The second school building on Church Street opposite St. Paul's Episcopal Church was used until the opening of the Old Norfolk Academy building on Bank Street in 1841, with John P. Scott, a fiery-tempered Irishman as its headmaster. Tradition says that when the weather was warm and the boys were obstreperous, Scott would swoop down on the culprits and toss them out of the nearest window.

Besides the Academy there were many other privately operated schools in Norfolk during the early Nineteenth Century, notably the Lancastrian School (1815-1856), one of the many monitor-operated, non-sectarian institutions of its kind in the United States, established by Joseph Lancaster (1778-1838), an English educator and a member of the Society of Friends.

All of these privately owned Norfolk schools operated on

a tuition basis, however, making it difficult for the average poor child to obtain even the rudiments of an education.

Finally this condition was changed in 1850, when Norfolk, by an act of the Virginia Assembly was authorized to establish a free public school system. It was not until 1858, however, that Norfolk's first four public schools for any white person between the ages of six and twenty-one were opened, with Thomas C. Tabb (1803-1873) as the city's first public school superintendent.

Chapter Fifty-four

Norfolk's Farewell to a Hero

When General Robert E. Lee visited Norfolk for the last time he was the guest of Dr. William Selden, the father of William Boswell Selden, the first Norfolk man killed in the Civil War. Young Selden was mortally wounded at Roanoke Island, N.C., on February 8, 1862.

General Lee had less than five months to live when he stepped off the train in Portsmouth on April 30, 1870. He was returning from a southern trip for the benefit of his health and was accompanied by his daughter, Miss Agnes Lee.

When it was learned that he was a passenger aboard the Seaboard & Roanoke Railroad train en route from Wilmington, N.C., to Portsmouth, the Norfolk area went wild with excitement. Thousands of admirers gathered at the depot to greet him. And when he emerged from the coach, the air resounded with one crescendo after another of rebel yells. Also on hand was a famous Confederate cannon, affectionately known as "Brick Pomeroy," which the Portsmouth Volunteer Fire Department had dragged to the station in order to greet "Marse Robert" with a volley of salvos.

Colonel Walter Herron Taylor, Lee's former aide-de-camp, met his old chief at the train and escorted him to Norfolk on the ferry, where Lee occupied a special cabin to avoid being exhausted by the people who wished to show him their gratitude and devotion.

As soon as the ferry left Portsmouth, fireworks were set off on its deck to let the people in Norfolk know that Lee was on the way, while the Union Fire Department of Norfolk took up the saluting with another cannon on Market Square where the ferry docked.

In Norfolk, Lee was greeted with more rebel yells as he was driven to the home of Dr. Selden at the southwest corner of Freemason and Botetourt streets.

The next day, a Sunday, Lee escorted Miss Caroline Selden, his host's youngest daughter, to Old Christ Church. The route through which the carriage passed was lined with Lee's old soldiers with their hats in their hands. That night Lee was entertained at an elaborate dinner party by William Eyre Taylor in his home on Bute Street, now the site of the Central YMCA.

Lee's health had not been improved by his southern trip, but he would not permit his host to forbid his former men from visiting him.

On Wednesday, May 4, 1870, after attending a service at St. Paul's Episcopal Church, Lee rested before the reception that his host had planned for him later that day.

That evening the Seldens' latchstring was on the outside, and Norfolk-area Confederate veterans from all walks of life waited patiently in line to shake the hand of their former beloved general. One of these was Bryan, Lee's faithful manservant of the war days. Also on hand was eighty-nine-year-old Emanuel J. Myers, who proudly wore the Legion of Honor which had been presented to him in his youth by Napoleon.

Before going to bed, Lee was given a physical examination by Dr. Selden, after which he fell asleep, weary but touched and full of memories, while the rain beat a ghostly tatoo on the rooftop.

The next day Lee and his daughter took a steamer for Lower Brandon, the Harrison plantation on the James River, where he rested for a few days before setting out on the last leg of his trip home to Lexington. Less than six months later, Norfolk again paid tribute to Lee, but that time the muffled tolling of bells replaced the booming of cannon and the chorus of rebel yells.

Lee had died on October 12, 1870, in Lexington, where, as the president of Washington College (later Washington and Lee University), he had spent his last years teaching, by example and precept, the youth of Virginia to be good Americans.

Chapter Fifty-five

The Norfolk Library and Its Antecedents

The Norfolk Public Library of today, incorporated by an Act of the Virginia Assembly in February of 1894, had one legitimate and several bar sinister antecedents.

Its legitimate ancestor was the Norfolk Library Association, organized on August 18, 1870, with Dr. Samuel Selden as its first president and T. B. West as its first librarian. Its books, contained in eight rows of shelves, and a varied selection of periodicals, were originally housed in the Old Norfolk Academy building on Bank Street.

The association's career was rather precarious. Depending on subscriptions, which were not always forthcoming, its road was hard. No new books, no new subscribers, no new subscribers, no new books — a somewhat hopeless circle.

The Act of the Assembly in 1894 ended this vicious pattern, however, and with it the Norfolk Public Library system of today was born.

Before the establishment of the Norfolk Library Association in 1870, there were several subscription circulating libraries in Norfolk, some of which had fairly active histories.

The first indication that Norfolk had a subscription library comes from the "American Journey — 1793-1798" by Moreau de St. Mery. In it he wrote: "Norfolk also has a book dealer who makes quite an advantageous affair out of the rental of books. This bookseller is M(r). Hunter."

Sometime before 1795, Hunter died, at which time his business was taken over by the Messrs. Rainbow and Hannah, stationers, who issued a catalog of the books in the library in 1796, a copy of which is preserved in the Sargeant Memorial Room of Kirn Memorial Library.

As far as can be ascertained, the Rainbow and Hannah subscription library was the only one of its kind in late Eighteenth Century Norfolk. But there were several excellent private libraries in the borough during the early years of the Nineteenth Century, notably those of Littleton Waller Tazewell and General Robert Barraud Taylor.

Norfolk's second subscription library belonged to the Norfolk Athenaeum, a "library company" chartered by the Virginia Assembly on January 5, 1816. General Robert Barraud Taylor was its first president, and one thousand five hundred dollars was appropriated for the purchase of books.

Each of the seventy-eight original members was assessed twenty-five dollars to cover the expenses, but some of them never paid their assessments, and this contributed to the failure of the undertaking. There also seems to have been no permanent place for the storage of the library's books, because each succeeding president moved the library to suit his convenience.

Finally, in 1842, the Norfolk Athenaeum went out of existence, and its library was sold at public auction.

Two other early Nineteenth Century Norfolk subscription libraries deserve mention.

On March 23, 1827, William Maxwell, a prominent Norfolk lawyer and later the editor of the Virginia Historical Register, opened the Norfolk Lyceum on Wolfe, later Market, Street.

The purpose of the Lyceum was to house a subscription library and to provide a meeting place for literary associations. It continued to operate until 1839, when it was sold to the Washington and Lafayette Odd Fellows Lodges. It burned on February 18, 1859.

The other subscription library was operated by the Washington Institute and Library Association. In 1853, the American Beacon carried a notice of the organization of this group, a venture that was short lived because of delinquent subscribers and the deaths of many of the paying members during the yellow fever epidemic of 1855.

Chapter Fifty-six

The Virginia Club

The Virginia Club, which still functions in quiet exclusiveness in its second-floor eyrie above the south entrance of the Selden Arcade, is Norfolk's oldest male coterie.

Its beginning, according to a copy of its constitution and bylaws published in 1891, dates from June of 1873, when a party of bon vivants met "by chance one evening" in the rooms of John Vermillion above Taylor's Drug Store at Bank and Freemason streets.

Mutually agreeing that Norfolk was badly in need of a silk stocking male refuge away from home, the group appointed a committee to look into the matter. By June 26, 1873, things had progressed so rapidly that the first meeting of the new club's board of directors was held, at which Colonel Walter Herron Taylor, General Lee's former aide-de-camp, was chosen president.

Strict deportment was stressed from the beginning, as the following excerpts culled at random from its bylaws show:

"Crockery and glassware, furniture, or other property of the Club, broken or injured by a member, must be paid for at the time."

"No dog shall be allowed in the Club house."

"No member will be permitted to lie or sleep on any sofa or lounge in the Club house."

During its existence, the club (its name was proposed by Frank Dornin, an original member) has occupied many buildings, notably its former ornate headquarters built in the early 1900s at the southwest corner of Granby and Plume streets.

Three years after its founding, the club celebrated its third anniversary with a gastronomic binge in its original club-rooms at 59 Main Street. And as January 8, 1876, the date of the banquet, fell on Saturday that year, allowing the members the weekend to recover from the Epicurean and Bacchanalian excesses of the night before, the caterer was given carte blanche when it came to preparing the menu.

Even a reading of the bill of fare that was printed in The Norfolk Virginian for January 9, 1876, is enough to set one's taste buds working overtime, while one is also inclined to speculate if any of the present members could survive for long after partaking a similar setup of edibles and beverages.

Things got under way with stewed Cherrystone oysters and raw and pickled bivalves from Lynnhaven and Horn Harbor. These were followed by baked Todd's old Smithfield hams, baked beef tongues, old Lane hams, and spiced rounds of Baltimore beef.

Then came the roasts — a saddle of mountain mutton, turkeys dressed with meat jelly, beef tongues a l'Escarlate, and ham au jus. These were followed in stately gastronomic procession by boned chicken in jelly, stewed terapins, mayonnaise of lobster, lobster a l'Indienne, and anchovy and chicken salads.

As if this wasn't enough, the waiters then brought in canvas-back ducks, blue-wing ducks, venison, and partridges on toast. And to provide zest to all the above, the caterer also provided ample supplies of celery, cole slaw, pepper sauce, London Club sauce, Worcestershire sauce, mixed pickles, chow chow, tomato catsup, English mustard, horse radish, English pickles, and French mustard.

Then when dessert time finally arrived, the tables were cleared and bowls of oranges, bananas, pears, apples, and Malaga and Isabella grapes were set out.

Last, but not least, all of the above was washed down with the best liquors ranging from cream-rich bourbon to vintage champagne.

Chapter Fifty-seven

General Pickett's Funeral

General George Edward Pickett, whose division made the famous charge at the Battle of Gettysburg, died on July 30, 1875, in St. Vincent de Paul Hospital at Wood and Church streets in Norfolk.

General Pickett, who was the Virginia agent for the Washington Life Insurance Co. at the time of his death, had been in Norfolk for several weeks. He was staying at the Atlantic Hotel on Main Street when he was stricken and was moved to the hospital where he could rest more quietly.

According to The Norfolk Virginian of July 31, 1875, General Pickett died at 10:45 p.m. on July 30, after which immediate plans were made to give him an elaborate funeral.

Born in Richmond on January 25, 1825, Pickett graduated from West Point in 1846 and saw service under General Winfield Scott in the Mexican War.

His great day, however, came on July 3, 1863, when he led fifteen thousand men in the daring assault on the Federal lines that is known in history as "the High Water Mark of the Confederacy."

General Pickett's funeral, one of the largest ever held in Norfolk, was described in detail in the August 1, 1875, issue of The Norfolk Virginian.

Although it was a hot day, East Freemason Street was crowded with spectators, while Old Christ Church, at the northwest corner of Freemason and Cumberland streets, where the funeral was held, was jammed to the doors.

The ceremony began when the Norfolk Light Artillery Blues, the Norfolk City Guard, the Grice Commandery of Knights Templars, and the Norfolk Fire Department, led by the Norfolk Post Band, escorted the body from the hospital to the church.

The eighteen pallbearers, headed by General William Mahone, Colonel Walter Herron Taylor, and General Richard Lucien Page, all distinguished Confederates, marched two by two on each side of the hearse.

This was followed by six "stalwart well-dressed colored men" who lifted the coffin from the hearse and bore it into the church under a glittering archway made by the crossed swords of the Knights Templars.

After the burial psalm was sung by the choir, the Reverend O. S. Barten, the rector of Christ Church, read the Episcopal burial service. This was followed by the singing of "Nearer, My God, to Thee," after which the Knights Templars conducted a ritual of their own.

Then the procession re-formed to go to Cedar Grove Cemetery.

Leading it was a platoon of Norfolk policemen, followed by the Norfolk Post Band playing dirges, the Norfolk Guards, and the Norfolk Light Artillery Blues.

Then came the hack containing the clergyman, followed by the Norfolk Fire Department on foot, the hearse, and carriages for the general's relatives and friends.

Pickett was temporarily buried in a vault in Cedar Grove Cemetery as it was not convenient at that time to take his body to Richmond. As no military salute was fired in Cedar Grove, The Virginian hastened to explain:

"In regard to the omission to fire the usual salute over the grave by the infantry, we have been requested to state that according to military etiquette such a salute would have barred any future military honors by the State to the illustrious dead. Of course, such honors will be tendered at the proper time."

Pickett's body was subsequently shipped to Richmond, where it was buried in Hollywood Cemetery on October 25, 1875, with full military honors.

Chapter Fifty-eight

The Russian Invasion

Norfolk society went into its dizziest tailspin in January of 1877, when the Russian Imperial Grand Dukes Alexis and Constantine and their suites paid the city a surprise visit.

Nothing like it had happened since Lady Dunmore showed the Norfolk provincials the latest minuet steps in 1774. By comparison, the much touted International Azalea Festivals of later years are like so many country church covered-dish suppers.

The noble globetrotters arrived in Norfolk aboard the Imperial Russian frigate Swetlana on January 13, 1877, and from then until the dukes departed for New York, Norfolk society had palpitations of the heart on a twenty-four-hour basis.

The bon ton of that period was so unused to imperial visitations that it even overlooked a slur aimed in its direction by the Grand Duke Alexis immediately after his arrival.

It was only twelve years after Appomattox, and the haute monde was still trying to recoup the family fortunes that had been considerably reduced during "The Late Unpleasantness."

When the Grand Duke Alexis learned that two of the top leaders of Norfolk society were in the grocery and auction business, he is reported to have raised his imperial eyebrows and remarked, "Really! Am I to be presented to Norfolk society by a grocer and be forced to dance with the wife of the town crier?"

But this jibe was forgotten temporarily in the whirlwind of pleasure kicked up by the imperial visit.

Theater parties at the Church Street Opera House, a Grand Complimentary German in the old Masonic Temple on Freemason Street, a Grand Naval Ball held in the flag-bedecked, flower-banked sail loft of the Norfolk Naval Shipyard, all climaxed by a Grand Matinee Dansante aboard the Swetlana, kept the Norfolk-area social scene in a tizzy for over a month.

In reporting the German, a Baltimore paper added this titillating note: "A young lady of Norfolk was so agitated while dancing with the Grand Duke that she fainted in his arms. The scion of nobility merely passed her over to one of the old ladies with the remark, "Too-damn-thin-o-vich!" and secured another partner."

Despite the frosting on the social cake, however, all was not well aboard the Swetlana, and most of the time while the Grand Dukes and the top Russian naval officers were cavorting ashore, the petty officers of the ship were having a time keeping the sailors from open mutiny.

The Norfolk police also had their hands full keeping the Russian sailors in line when they were on shore leave. Saloon keepers continued serving the drunken sailors on their way back to the ship, and in some instances these establishments even kept their rear doors open for the Russians when the saloons were supposed to be closed, all of which brought a severe rebuke from the civil authorities.

Many stories have come down from the time of the imperial visit, but the following is indicative of what the high-born Russian visitors were doing when they were not tripping the light fantastic.

On one occasion, when the Grand Duke Alexis was scheduled to attend a fashionable affair in Portsmouth, he was not to be found. Finally a search party composed of a number of leading citizens tracked him down behind a high board fence on the farm of John Edwards, an eccentric bachelor. They discovered His Imperial Highness perched on top of a barrel watching a cockfight!

Chapter Fifty-nine

The Negro in Norfolk

Although it has not always been acknowledged, the Negro has played an important role in the development of Norfolk since its establishment.

The strength and endurance of Negro men provided the main source of manpower to load and unload the vessels that brought prosperity to the area, while other members of the race faithfully served the private families and public and religious establishments of the growing town, borough, and city as clergymen, teachers, cooks, butlers, waiters, housemaids, nurses, washerwomen, and coachmen.

Members of the black race also distinguished themselves in time of war. For instance, James Thomas, a Norfolk Negro, served with distinction as a boatswain during the Revolutionary War in the Virginia Navy and was described as a "fellow of daring and, though a man of color, was respected by all the officers who served with him."

Norfolk also had the distinction of having the most publicized school for Negro children prior to the Civil War. It was established by Mrs. Margaret Douglass, a white woman from South Carolina, who opened classes in Norfolk in 1853 for free Negro children. Arrested on the charge that slaves were among her pupils. Mrs. Douglass denied her guilt, but was found guilty and sentenced to one month in the Norfolk City Jail, an episode that received national publicity in a book published in 1854.

Norfolk's first free public schools for Negroes were opened in 1863 in schools formerly used by white children by order of the Federal occupation forces. In 1865, the Norfolk schools were returned to the use of the white children, and Negro children in the city were without schools until 1867, when the American Missionary Society opened several Negro schools in the city. This arrangement continued until 1871, when the City Council established a free Negro school in each of the four city wards and combined all of the schools, white and black, under one superintendent.

Higher education for Negroes came to Norfolk in 1883, when the Norfolk Mission College, which continued until 1916, was established by the General Assembly of the Presbyterian Church.

Norfolk's first Negro newspaper was published by Joseph T. Wilson, a runaway Norfolk slave, who returned from South America to the United States to enlist in the Union Army at the outbreak of the Civil War. Wilson became the editor of the True Southerner in Norfolk in 1866, which he continued to publish until a white Norfolk mob smashed his presses, after which he continued his newspaper career in Petersburg.

In the realm of religion, Norfolk's Negro Baptists have the oldest history. Norfolk's first Baptist congregation, organized in 1800, was interracial and worshiped in the then abandoned Norfolk Borough Church, now St. Paul's Episcopal Church. In 1815, the white members withdrew and founded Cumberland Street Baptist Church, the mother church of all white Baptist congregations in Norfolk. The Negro members, served by a white minister, the Reverend James Mitchell, an Englishman, continued as an independent congregation and became the progenitor of First Baptist Church, Bute Street, and Bank Street Baptist Church of today.

Grace Episcopal Church, originally called The Church of the Holy Innocents, was founded in 1883 by Negroes who had been communicants of Old Christ Church. Norfolk's Negro Catholics also worshipped with white Catholics until 1889, when St. Joseph's Parish was established for them. Since 1961, they have worshipped in Old St. Mary's Catholic Church.

Norfolk's oldest Negro Methodist church, St. John African Methodist Episcopal Church, was an outgrowth of a mission for slaves established by Cumberland Street Methodist Church in 1840. The present congregation still occupies the site on Bute Street bought for its original church in 1848.

The United Order of Tents, J. R. G. and J. U., one of the most important Negro women's lodges in the country, was also founded in Norfolk by two slave women, Annetta M. Lane of Norfolk and Harriet R. Taylor of Hampton, with the aid of two abolitionists, Joshua R. Giddings and Joliffe Union, whose initials are incorporated in the lodge title. Set up originally as an underground railway for slaves, the lodge threw off its secrecy after the Civil War and was officially organized in Norfolk in 1867.

Chapter Sixty

Norfolk and the Revolutionary Centennial

If it hadn't been for Michael Glennan (1844-1899), the owner and editor of The Norfolk Virginian, the original ancestor of The Virginian-Pilot, there might never have been a national centennial celebration at Yorktown in 1881 or a permanent marble monument at the same place commemorating the surrender of Cornwallis to the American and French forces one hundred years earlier.

Glennan, who began his career as a poor immigrant boy from Maynooth, County Kildare, Ireland, became the sole proprietor of The Virginian on March 24, 1876, when he was thirty two. One year earlier, after the celebration of the centennial of the Battle of Bunker Hill, he began a one-man campaign to promote a similar celebration at Yorktown in 1881.

In 1878, Glennan began a correspondence with Hugh Blair Grigsby, the president of the Virginia Historical Society and the chancellor of the College of William and Mary, to promote the project. When this led to no definite conclusion because of Grigsby's failing health, Glennan decided to advocate publicly the proposed celebration in the editorial columns of his newspaper.

On July 8, 1878, The Virginian commented: "The 19th of October 1881, will be the centennial anniversary of the capture of Cornwallis, and the American nation owes it to itself and the memory of the men who achieved its liberties, that it should be celebrated with a pomp and circumstance worthy of the event it commemorates."

Glennan's personal crusade in The Virginian was hailed enthusiastically by the nation's press and resulted in a meeting of the governors of the thirteen original states in Independence Hall in Philadelphia on October 18, 1879. At that time, Governor Frederick W. M. Holliday of Virginia appointed Glennan, who was present, as commissioner to represent Virginia in appreciation of his services.

In that capacity, Glennan participated prominently on October 23, 1879, at a preliminary celebration at Yorktown, at which time he offered the unanimously adopted resolutions that instructed John Goode, the Virginia representative in Congress from the district that included Yorktown, to request the government to appropriate funds to erect a Yorktown Victory Monument and to plan for a four-day national celebration of the surrender of Cornwallis to take place at Yorktown in October of 1881.

In view of the enthusiastic national endorsement of the

project that had originally been spearheaded and fostered by Glennan, Congress rose handsomely to the occasion and appropriated the funds for the monument, the erection of which had been considered by that body as early as October 29, 1781.

The centennial celebration at Yorktown on October 18-21, 1881, in which Glennan played a prominent part, was presided over by President Chester A. Arthur and was attended by notables from at home and abroad as well as thousands of patriotic citizens from all over the country.

On the Norfolk aspect of the celebration, Robert W. Lamb, editor of "Our Twin Cities of the Nineteenth Century: (Norfolk and Portsmouth) Their Past, Present and Future" (1887-88), wrote:

"On October 11 a proclamation by the Mayor requested an active participation by all citizens in a week of festivities from Monday, the 15th. He specially included the large fleet of British vessels lying at our wharves to participate in this celebration, as they gave our port 'a great victory of peace, instead of the dread alarm of war which the British fleet created one hundred years ago.'

"It was a sight," Lamb continued, "to see the throngs by day wending their way through the triumphal arches adorned with appropriate mottoes and pictures, but a greater sight at night, in the full glare of the electric light, introduced into our city for the first time to grace the occasion, the old and staid citizen vieing with the child in merry amusement to honor our great centennial."

Bibliography

In writing this book I have consulted the original sources as far as possible for my facts. These are the records of Lower Norfolk County now preserved in the Circuit Court of the City of Chesapeake; the Norfolk Council Orders for 1736-1798; and the wills, deeds, marriage bonds and other records of the Corporation Court of the City of Norfolk.

I have also used extensively the microfilm files of the late Eighteenth and early Nineteenth Century Norfolk newspapers as well as those of the Virginia Gazette on file in the Sargeant Memorial Room of Kirn Memorial Library.

Other collective printed sources used by me from the same collection were the bound volumes of the *Lower Norfolk County Antiquary, Virginia Magazine of History and Biography, William and Mary College Quarterly*, and *Virginia Historical Register*, as well as early Norfolk borough and city directories dating from 1801 through 1881.

The principal printed sources used by me, most of them part of the Sargeant Memorial Room collection at Kirn Memorial Library are:

Bailey, James Henry III: *A History of the Diocese of Richmond.* Richmond, Va., 1956.

Burton, Harrison W. ("Harry Scratch") : *The History of Norfolk, Virginia.* Norfolk, Va., 1877.

Calendar of Virginia State Papers and Other Manuscripts, 1652-1869. Richmond, Va., 1875-1893, 11 vols.

Centenary Souvenir of St. Mary's Church. Norfolk, 1958.

Cross, Charles B., Jr.: *The County Court, 1637-1904, Norfolk County, Virginia.* Portsmouth, Va., 1964.

Cross, Charles B., Jr.: *The Chesapeake: A Biography of a Ship.* Chesapeake, Va., 1968.

Dictionary of American Biography. Dumas Malone, editor. New York, N.Y., 1936.

Eckenrode, H. J.: *The Revolution in Virginia.* New York, N.Y., 1916.

Encyclopedia of Virginia Biography. Lyon Gardner Tyler, editor. New York, N.Y., 1915.

Fitzpatrick, John C.: *George Washington, Colonial Traveller (1732-1775)*. Indianapolis, Ind., 1927.

Forrest, William S.: *Historical and Discriptive Sketches of Norfolk and Vicinity*. Philadelphia, Pa., 1853.

Hening, William W.: *The Statutes at Large Being a Collection of all the Laws of Virginia From the First Session of the Legislature, in the Year 1619*. Richmond, Va., 1809-1823.

Jester, Annie Lash and Hiden, Martha Woodroof: *Adventures of Purse and Person*. 1956, (second edition), 1964.

Lorant, Stefan: *The New World*. New York, N.Y., 1943.

Noel Hume, Ivor: *1775 - Another Part of the Field*. New York, N.Y., 1966.

Read, Helen Calvert Maxwell, (1750-1833): *Memoirs of Helen Calvert Maxwell Read*. Charles B. Cross, Jr., editor. Chesapeake, Va., 1970.

Rorer, Henry S.: *History of Norfolk Public Schools*. Typescript copy in Sargeant Memorial Room, Kirn Memorial Library. Norfolk, Va., 1968.

Smith, John: *Captain John Smith, Travels and Works*. Edward Arber, editor. Edinburgh, Scotland, 1910.

Squires, W. H. T.: Scrapbooks in Sargeant Memorial Room, Kirn Memorial Library, Norfolk, containing articles on Norfolk history published in the Norfolk Ledger-Dispatch, 1935-1948.

Stern, Dr. Malcolm H.: *Some Notes on the History of the Organized Jewish Community of Norfolk*. The Journal of the Southern Jewish Historical Society, November, 1963.

Stern, Dr. Malcolm H.: *Moses Myers and the Early Jewish Community of Norfolk*. The Journal of the Southern Jewish Historical Society, November, 1958.

Stewart, William H.: *History of Norfolk County, Virginia, and Representative Citizens*. Chicago, Ill., 1902.

Wertenbaker, Thomas Jefferson: *Norfolk: Historic Southern Port*. Durham, N.C., 1931. Second Edition, edited by Marvin W. Schlegel, 1962.

Whichard, Rogers Dey: *History of Lower Tidewater Virginia*. New York, N.Y., 1959.

Writers Program of the Works Progress Administration in the State of Virginia: *The Negro in Virginia*. New York, N.Y., 1940.

Index

Point Comfort, 4, 92
Poole, Edward, 63; Sarah, 63
Porter, Capt. David, 88-89
Portsmouth, 23, 27, 43, 56, 65, 67-69, 71, 73, 75-76, 110-111, 120
Portsmouth ferry terminal, 70
Portsmouth Naval Hospital, 12, 62
Portsmouth Volunteer Fire Department, 110
Post Office (Norfolk), 81
Powell, Nathaniel, 3
Powhatan, 2
Powhatan Confederacy, 2
Presbyterian General Assembly, 55, 121
Presbyterians, 54-56, 104-105
Press Gang, 25-26
Princess Anne County, 85
Princess Anne Road, 99, 102
Printing, 39-41
Profit, Jonas, 3
Public Wharf, 25
Purdie, George, 81

Quashabee, 24

Rainbow and Hannah, Messrs, 113
Raleigh Avenue, 103
Raleigh, Sir Walter, 1-2
Randolph, Sir John, 17; John of Roanoke, 106
Read, Mrs. Helen Calvert Maxwell, 23, 87; Dr. John K., 34
"Recruiting Officer", 50
Register, Joshua, 105
Reinsburg, John, 28
Revolutionary War, 44-45
Richmond, 67-68, 73-74, 79-80, 98-99, 116, 118
Riddick, Col. Edward, 27
Rip Raps (Castle Calhoun), 67, 94
Roanoke Island (N.C.), 1, 110
Robinson, Capt. William, 14
Roosevelt, Theodore, 82
Roman Catholic Society (Norfolk), 77

St. John AME Church, 122
St. Joseph's Parish, 122
St. Louis (Mo.), 71
St. Mary's Catholic Church, 77-78, 105, 122
St. Mery, Moreau de, 113
St. Patrick's Catholic Church, 72, 74, 77
St. Paul's Boulevard, 3, 29, 108
St. Paul's Churchyard, 18, 31, 33
St. Paul's Episcopal Church (Borough Church), 28-29, 32-33, 35, 43, 83, 87, 104, 109, 111, 121
St. Paul's Episcopal Church (Richmond), 98
St. Vincent de Paul Hospital, 116
Sale, John M., 103
Sanborn, Lt. A. L., 95-96
Santo Domingo, 46
Saunders, Miss Elizabeth Selden (Bettie), 98-99; Capt. John L., 98; Mrs. Martha Bland Selden, 98
Schisano, M., 79
"School for Scandal", 52
Schools (White), 108-110; (Negro), 121
Scott, John P., 109; Gen. Winfield, 107, 116
Seabury, Capt. F. W., 36
Seaboard & Roanoke Railroad, 110
Seal, Norfolk Borough, (1740), 18; (1741), 19; Norfolk City, 13
Seawell, Henry, 6
Selden Arcade, 114
Selden House, 82
Selden, Miss Caroline, 111; Dr. Samuel, 112; Dr. William, 82, 110-111; Dr. William Boswell, 82; William Boswell, 110
Sewells Point, 4, 6, 31, 92-94
Sewells Point, Battle of, 91-93
Ships: Adelaide, 94; Baltimore, 95; Ben Franklin, 72-73; Centipede, 65; Chesapeake, 60-61; J. E. Coffee, 74; Concord, 106; Constellation, 63-64; Constitution, 60; Delaware, 107; Elizabeth, 11;

Essex, 88; Hornet, 25; Huis van Nassau, 10; L'Andromede, 107; Leopard, 60-61; Liverpool, 36; Merrimack (Virginia), 62, 91, 93, 95; Miami, 94; Mississippi, 88; Monitor, 91, 93-95; Monticello, 92-93; Pennsylvania, 90, Petersburg, 66; Potomac, 68; Prosperous, 5, 9; Swetlana, 118-119; Ville de Paris, 28

Sickelmore, Michael, 3

Simmons's Directories (1801 and 1806-07), 47-48

Singleton, William R., 71

Skicoak, 1-2, 9

Smith, Capt. John, 2-4; Peter, 11; Samuel the elder (Mr. Sam), 16, 18, 108; Samuel the younger, 18

Sons of Liberty, 51

"Stabat Mater" (Rossini), 49

Stamp Act, 51

Stanton, Edwin M., 94

"Star Spangled Banner", 59

Stern, Dr. Malcolm H., 101-103

Stingray Point, 3

Stockley Gardens, 103-104

Storms (Hurricanes), 5-6, 84

Strachey, William, 2

Streets; Bank, 55, 71, 101, 104, 107, 112, 114; Bermuda, 14, 52; Botetourt, 30, 82, 111; Boush, 29; Brewer, 85; Bute, 30, 82, 111, 122; Catharine, 55, 104; Chapel, 77; Charlotte, 30, 55, 104; Church, 29, 33, 62, 73, 96, 102, 107-109, 116; Cumberland, 30, 43, 81, 103-104, 117; Duke, 30, 81-82; Dunmore, 30; East, 14, 67; Fenchurch, 30, 43, 52; Freemason, 30, 38, 81-82, 84, 101, 104, 111, 114, 117; Granby, 30-31, 115; Grafton, 82; Gunpowder, 31; Holt, 77; Main, 12, 14, 29, 42, 50, 53, 58-59, 67-68, 71-72, 96, 107; Market, 90, 102, 114; Plume, 53, 115; Water, 58; Wide Water, 57; Wolfe, 90, 102, 114; Wood, 116; Yarmouth, 30; York, 30

Stuart, Prince Charles, 5; Prince Charles Edward, 30, 40; Princess Elizabeth, 5; Prince Henry, 5; John (Third Earl of Bute), 30

Suffolk, 28, 68

Swindells, James H., 49

Sykes, Pvt. Alexander, 93

Tabb, Thomas C., 110

Tappan, J. Nelson, 80

Taylor, Harriet R., 122; Dr. James, 34; John, 18, 34; Gen. Robert Barraud, 63, 65-67, 113; Richard, 82; Robert, 34; Col. Walter Herron, 98-99, 110, 114, 117; William Eyre, 111

Taylor's Drug Store, 114

Taylor-Whittle House, 81

Tazewell, Littleton W., 59, 82, 113

Tents, United Order of, 122

Theaters: Academy of Music, 53-54; Avon, 52; Calvert's Lane, 52; "Capt. Newton's Great Room", 50, 52; Church Street Opera House (Norfolk Varieties), 49, 53, 119; Colonial, 82; Fenchurch Street, 62; Gaiety, 49, 53; King's Lane (Norfolk's first), 50-52; Mechanic's Hall, 49, 53

Theseum (Athens), 81

Thimble Shoals Channel, 60

Thomas, James, 120

Thompson's Stage, 68

Thorowgood, Capt. Adam, 6-9, 68

Tidewater Drive, 102

"To Anacreon in Heaven", 59

Todkill, Anas, 3

Town Point, 12, 29, 31

"Towne of Lower Norfolk County" (Norfolk Towne), 7, 13

Treaty of Paris (1783), 56

Trige, Paul, 12

Trinity Churchyard (Portsmouth), 56

"True Southerner", 121

Tucker, John, 34; Robert I, 18; Robert II, 18